The Dunblane Centre
The Gift That Keeps Growing

Published by
Jamieson and Munro

ISBN No.
978-0-9553057-9-5

Printed by
The Monument Press, Abbey Road, Riverside, Stirling FK8 1LP

DEDICATION

This book is dedicated to the memory of Gwen Mayor and all of the children who lost their lives at Dunblane Primary School in March 1996, to the children and teachers who were injured that day and to everyone from near and far whose response to the Tragedy has ensured that Dunblane was able to recover with dignity and pride.

The book is also a tribute to every single person who has participated in the life of The Centre since its inception. We pay a special tribute to Chris Finnerty, a DC trustee who sadly died whilst this book was being prepared.

All Profits from the sale of the Book will be used to support the Dunblane Centre which is operated by the Dunblane Youth and Sports Centre Trust, a charity registered in Scotland, SC027397.

*This book has been produced by Jamieson & Munro
and production costs were supported
by a grant from the
Trustees of the John Jamieson Munro Charitable Trust*

CONTENTS

FOREWORD

ANDY MURRAY

Dunblane is my hometown, the place where I grew up, where I went to school and where I learned to play tennis. In March 1996 the primary school I attended witnessed a tragedy, which I can never forget and will always find difficult to talk about and comprehend. But following such a dreadful event the community of Dunblane found a purpose and determination, which everyone associated with the town, past and present, can always be proud of.

The town received support from the widest possible community, one that extended far beyond my hometown. Gifts were sent from across Scotland, from throughout the UK and from all around the world, donations given by people whose love and support flooded into the town. And it is from the generosity shown by that global community that the Dunblane Centre evolved.

Those who watch the news when Jamie or I are competing in grand slams will have seen the local community cheering us on when live coverage is being screened at The Centre. But there's far more to The Centre than this. It is an impressive and unique community facility. This book records how The Centre evolved and how it has provided not only something from which the young people of Dunblane will continue to benefit over many years but a project that demonstrates the most positive response possible following a terrible tragedy.

Dunblane can be proud of its Centre and I am proud to be part of its
Tenth Anniversary.

(l) Andy and Jamie Murray; (r) The Olympic Gold Medal Winner Returns to Dunblane.
(Photo: PA)

CHAPTER 1 – A CAUSE FOR UNITY

LORD MICHAEL FORSYTH and LORD GEORGE ROBERTSON

Out of tragedy came hope. Out of generosity came the Dunblane Centre. Born of global sympathy it is the future and its anniversary is a tribute to that hope. As patrons we wish it well in its valuable role and mission and congratulate those who made it happen.

We are two politicians of different persuasions. One of us lived in Dunblane. The other represented the town in Parliament. One was Secretary of State for Scotland, the other was his Shadow.

Michael Forsyth and George Robertson with the Queen and the Princess Royal in Dunblane – March 1996. (Photo: Daily Rocord)

Politics in Scotland is a rough game. Views are held with passion. Normal restraint can be taken to the edge. No holds are barred. For the two of us personal and political differences were marked. We both led tribal forces.

After March 1996 we were changed for ever. Fused by the events we witnessed and experienced, our immediate resolve to respond in public together, and only together, had a remarkable national effect. We had no differences, no contrasting opinion, no competition, and political battles and argument were subordinated totally. People locally and much wider noticed and it mattered and it helped.

The Centre brings us together again. The vitality and energy of those who run and benefit from The Centre represent the promise of the future. Young people learn and enjoy. They come and take part. Activities enrol talent and vitality and people leave enriched.

Both of us have, for example, enjoyed the annual Burns Supper – run exclusively by the youngsters. We were bowled over by the product of the efforts put in. Poetry and song were brought to life by a new generation tutored by committed leaders like Nancy McLaren.

The Centre has grown from just a good idea to being a means of fulfilling a clear local need. It has also, through the insight, dynamism and dedication of the staff and supporters, become a local institution. Its reach has inspired and energised a new generation of Dunblane youth to see a wider, more satisfying world. That is indeed a huge achievement.

It has even had a national role. As a venue for the public supporting of Andy Murray it has projected pride and backing for a world-famous local boy. He is a role model to so many young people and the fact that his roots are in Dunblane and his successful career started here can encourage others to also reach for the stars.

The Dunblane Centre already helps young people to discover their talents and, who knows, with The Centre's help there may be more Andys ready to take off.

We wish The Centre more and more success.

Our Patrons at The Dunblane Centre –
June 2014.

CHAPTER 2 –
THE WORLD SENDS ITS LOVE TO DUNBLANE

MICK NORTH
with contributions from PAM ROSS and NORA GILFILLAN

DUNBLANE - SATURDAY 25 SEPTEMBER 2004

The Dunblane Centre Opening Ceremony – Mick North, Patron.

It's an uplifting image, white doves emerging from their basket to mark a flying start to Dunblane's brand new venture. It was a special day for a town which, eight and half years earlier, had faced the worst possible nightmare. The path that led to The Centre's Opening had begun with the terrible tragedy at Dunblane Primary School on 13 March 1996. Now, through the generosity of a worldwide public and the considerable dedication and work of many in the local community, the doves were symbolic of Dunblane's recovery and of the love and support it received during those darkest hours.

DUNBLANE - WEDNESDAY 13 MARCH 1996

This was the day that had changed Dunblane, the dreadful day when a suicidal man armed with four handguns walked unchallenged into the local primary school and, in a period lasting little more than three minutes, shot dead a teacher and sixteen of the 5- and 6-year-olds in her class and shot and injured ten more children and three teachers. A quiet Scottish town was left traumatised.

Primary 1/13: (l) Class Photo with teacher Gwen Mayor; (r) in December 1995.
(Photos: Whyler Photos, Jacqui Young)

Suddenly Dunblane was a name known everywhere, a town forever linked to a horrifying act which deprived it of so many of its precious children and a dedicated teacher. A ripple effect spread out far and wide from central Scotland. Those who saw the smiling faces of our children asked the same unanswerable question "Why?", and their response was immense.

People across the globe, trying to come to terms with something so awful and seemingly inexplicable, reached out to the Families and the Community. The huge shock and horror produced an outpouring of sympathy and support for Dunblane. The town became a focus for the love, kindness and generosity that so many people display when a catastrophic event strikes their fellow human beings.

This book tells the story of the **Dunblane Centre**, a very special legacy made possible by the public's generous cash donations in 1996. However, giving money was just one of the many ways in which people responded, and we could not overlook the myriad of other gifts received by the town. The huge scale of the response makes it impossible to record all but a very small proportion of that wealth of generosity for which the people of Dunblane will always be grateful. Those we do include must serve to represent all the acts of kindness, every gift received and each thought and prayer. Thank you all.

THE RESPONSE IN DUNBLANE

At a time when Dunblane was learning to cope with a media invasion and hosting visits from Royal and political dignitaries, its citizens reached out to those of us who were coming to terms with the death of a loved one or were anxiously caring for injured family members. A special Mass was held at the Church of the Holy Family, when a message from Pope John Paul II was read, and two days after the shootings hundreds and hundreds of people lined up to attend a vigil at Dunblane Cathedral. The weekend service at the Cathedral, on what so cruelly was Mothering Sunday, was broadcast by the BBC, and viewers would have felt the pain being suffered by the Community expressed so articulately by the minister Colin McIntosh. Within the next five days there would be seventeen funerals.

Later in the year, on 9 October, a Memorial Service was held at Dunblane Cathedral and also shown on BBC TV. By then it had become possible to contemplate a theme of 'Out of Darkness into Light'. Attended by the Prince of Wales, it was a poignant occasion, but one marked by a positivity and brightness which accompanied so many of the responses to a dark event. Our invited guest Lorraine Kelly read out the children's and Gwen

The Candles lit at the Memorial Service – October 1996.
(Photo: Chris Bacon)

Mayor's names as each family in turn lit a special personalised candle. Lorraine later wrote in her autobiography that "The lighting of the candles was to symbolise hope, and especially the hope that the whole community would now take its first steps out of darkness into light".

We know that around the country and across the world other services were held to remember our loved ones at the time of the Tragedy and later on other special occasions. In Dunblane, the Church of the Holy Family continues to hold a special Mass on each anniversary.

Flowers – Within hours of the Tragedy flowers were being placed in Doune Road beside the entrances to the Primary School, and over the next few days the floral bank grew and grew as townsfolk and visitors came to pay their respects and reflect on what had happened. The flowers were later transferred by volunteers to the town's cemetery – many people still recall the eerie rustle as a sea of cellophane shivered in the chilly March wind.

The Flowers outside Dunblane Primary School – March 1996.

5

Dunblane Cemetery – March 1996.

The Drop-In Centre and Support Centre – Those who were most directly affected by the Tragedy were given the support of the local authority and aided by family liaison teams. Communication within the Community came through a number of avenues. The Dunblane Community Council issued Emergency Newsletters and then Stirling Council provided regular Dunblane Updates, six issues being published between April 1996 and February 1997.

A Drop-In Centre, manned with trained counsellors and volunteers, was set up almost immediately, initially in Springbank Gardens and then in the High Street, and remained open for six months. It was estimated that thousands of people dropped in to look at the cards and books of condolences or to have a chat and a cup of tea. Hundreds of volunteers gave freely of their time with a warmth and spirit that matched the occasion and the mood.

The Support Centre arrived very quickly at the Braeport Centre as part of the Council's plans to provide support services to the individuals and the communities affected by the Tragedy. The staff were involved in a whole host of practical tasks ranging from passing on information and gifts, to advocating on behalf of individuals and groups and making the occasional cup of tea or coffee for those who'd called in. It supported the Community for nearly five years.

In recognition of their response to the Tragedy, the citizens of Dunblane received the 'People of the Year Award' at the Great Scots Awards in November 1996.

Rev Colin McIntosh (l) receives the 'People of the Year' Award from the Chair of Judges, Lord McClusky.
(Photo: Daily Record)

GIFTS AND MESSAGES FROM AROUND THE WORLD

Within days hundreds of messages were arriving in Dunblane in the form of letters and cards, together with books of condolence, some addressed to individual families, some to the School and some to the town. And this was perhaps the first occasion, at a time when the internet was a novelty and social media unknown, that condolence messages were being posted online. A collection of these was downloaded and bound copies made. Public figures around the world expressed their sympathy, many of their messages recorded for posterity in official documents.

 Congressional Record

United States of America

PROCEEDINGS AND DEBATES OF THE *104th* CONGRESS, SECOND SESSION

Vol. 141 — WASHINGTON, THURSDAY, MARCH 14, 1996 — No. 31

Senate

THE TRAGEDY IN DUNBLANE

Mr. WELLSTONE. Mr. President, I will be very brief. I actually do not have any prepared remarks, but I was thinking that maybe later on I would write up a resolution, or the leadership could write up some words, some kind of statement by the United States Senate, maybe it is a message of love, to the people of Dunblane, Scotland.

The slaughter of 16 children is just the ultimate nightmare. All of us who have children or grandchildren -- or whether we have or do not have children or grandchildren, it does not make any difference -- just in terms of our own humanity, I think we all can feel, and we know the horror of what has happened.

So, as a Senator from Minnesota, I just wanted to send my prayers and my love to the people of Dunblane and to tell them that today, in the U.S. Senate, it is not as if they are not in our thoughts and prayers.

Mr. President, I wish it was in my power to do more. I wish it was in our power to do more. But I think something should be said about it on the floor of the Senate, so I rise to speak, to send my love to the people of Scotland. I believe I speak for other Senators as well. Maybe later on today we can have a resolution that I know all of us will support.

Sometimes when you do this it seems unimportant, but it really is not, because it is kind of a way in which all the people of the world reach out and hug one another at these moments. So, later on, maybe we can have a leadership resolution or some kind of resolution that all Senators can sign on to, and we can send that to the parents, to the families of Dunblane.

I hope and pray this never happens again.

 Congressional Record

United States of America

PROCEEDINGS AND DEBATES OF THE *104th* CONGRESS, SECOND SESSION

Vol. 141 — WASHINGTON, THURSDAY, MARCH 14, 1996 — No. 31

Senate

SYMPATHIES TO THE PEOPLE OF SCOTLAND

Mr. WELLSTONE. Mr. President, while I have the floor, I do not want to interrupt if there are other Senators with amendments. I want them to have an opportunity to offer them. If not, let me just take a moment to read a resolution that has been accepted on both sides extending sympathies to the people of Scotland: [S2067]

Whereas, all Americans were horrified by the news this morning that 16 kindergarten children and their teacher were shot and killed yesterday in Dunblane, Scotland, by an individual who invaded their school;

Whereas, another 12 children and 3 adults were apparently wounded in the same terrible assault;

Whereas, this was an unspeakable tragedy of huge dimensions causing tremendous feeling of horror and anger and sadness affecting all people around the world;

And, whereas, the people of the United States wish to extend their sympathy to the people of Scotland in their hours of hurt, pain, and grief;

Therefore, be it resolved by the Senate of the United States that the Senate on behalf of the American people does extend its condolences and sympathies to the families of the little children and others who were murdered and wounded, and to all the people of Scotland with fervent hopes and prayers that such an occurrence will never ever again take place.

Mr. President, I wanted to read this on the floor. This has been accepted. This is the unanimous voice of the U.S. Senate.

I wish there was more that we could do. But I think it is important that we recognize what has happened and send our love and our support.

Mr. President, I yield the floor.

Messages from the US Senate, 14 March 1996, spoken by Senator Paul Wellstone, Minnesota, were sent to Dunblane.

The town's postal service had to adjust to a huge influx of extra mail, and those of us who received so many of the letters will always be grateful to the staff for how they dealt with it all. Sadly not all the letters were well meant, and the arrival of a handful of hate mail and other inappropriate communications placed an additional burden on the system with some of the Families' post initially being screened. Many volunteers helped to handle everything that was flooding into the town, opening envelopes and sorting the gifts. There were times when the number of letters was overwhelming with thousands upon thousands in black bags filling a unit on a local industrial estate. The first Dunblane Update described "the sheer volume of letters, cards, toys and other items the town has received" as staggering. My own experience during those first weeks was of dozens of letters arriving at the house each day. One day I counted more than 150. I read them all and the majority were kind, loving and very supportive. Some correspondents wanted to share a past experience of their own, and I was never sure what impact reading such deeply personal information might have on me, sometimes comforting though now and again causing additional pain. Some of us with no faith struggled with the religious messages, though I know many of these did bring comfort to other families.

Gifts received by the town were exhibited at the Drop-In Centre, and over the months they were put on public display in local halls. After Easter the town's children were invited to take home soft toys donated to Dunblane. A list of Gifts and Tributes compiled by Stirling Council in December 1996 included, among the hundreds of items received, samplers, plaques, photographs, quilts and other handmade items like blankets, embroidery and tapestries. There were religious gifts in the form of prayers, crosses, candles, bibles and other spiritual texts. Many framed items were sent, including letters, drawings, pictures, certificates and needlework, and there were larger paintings and artwork some reflecting the thoughts of whole communities. Vases, plates and a glass goblet had been generously given.

The Families were particularly taken with two special items of exceptional craftsmanship. Prisoners and officers at Craiginches Prison in Aberdeen made a beautiful grandfather clock which was kept in the lounge at Scottish Churches House in Dunblane where the Families were meeting each week. 'The Crystal Tree', an impressive seven-foot wrought iron structure decorated with crystals representing the Dunblane victims was delivered in person from Liverpool, although its exact provenance remains something of a mystery. It has had a number of homes over the years but is now, like the grandfather clock, being cared for by Old Churches House.

Special Gifts: The Grandfather Clock and 'The Crystal Tree'.

There were offers of a variety of holidays and short breaks for those most affected by the Tragedy. These came courtesy of both individuals and organisations like the Round Table and Rotary Club, and from home and abroad. With the support of Pedigree Petfoods a Dunblane pet shop arranged a winter trip to Aviemore, and the Celtic Supporters Club hosted Christmas Parties for Dunblane children in 1996 and 1997. It was not always easy to take advantage of such generous offers at a time when so many other things were going on. Bottles of champagne were sent from a vineyard in England. There were opportunities to have our loved ones portrayed in paintings. Caring treatments like hand massage, aromatherapy, homeopathy and Shen therapy were made available to the Families. The wider community too was able to share in some of these. Indeed there were numerous offers of practical help to the town in the aftermath of the Tragedy.

Gifts sent to Dunblane – displayed at St Blane's Church Hall.

Words and Music – Many people, amateurs and professionals, were inspired to write and compose. Books of new poems were sent, and there were copies of others already written, including the very special 'Andrew Poems' by Shelley Wagner from Virginia, a collection of poignant poems she had written about her son who had died in an accident, an individual copy sent to each of the bereaved families. Shelley later visited the Families in Dunblane. Another poem received by the Families 'Little Child Lost' was read at the Memorial Service by Lorraine Kelly. Recorded musical items both classical and contemporary were sent on tape and CD, and even sheet music arrived, and over the years we have learnt of other new music for Dunblane, such as 'The Little Ones' by Yusuf Islam (Cat Stevens), which he dedicated to the children of Sarajevo and Dunblane, and 'Child's Prayer' by James MacMillan which is on an album by The Sixteen, 'Bright Orb of Harmony'.

Just a few of the CDs of Songs written and recorded as a Tribute to the Dunblane Victims – these are from the UK, Germany and USA.

Around the world concerts were held in memory of the victims and many of these were recorded onto tapes and CDs and sent to the town. During the forthcoming months special musical events were organised in Dunblane and Stirling. Chris de Burgh gave a concert at Stirling Castle in aid of the Dunblane Fund, a pipe band marched through Dunblane and a group of professional country and western stars from Australia played a Down Under Country Music Concert, 'An Evening of Country Music for Dunblane' at Stirling's Albert Halls. As part of a short tour in May 1997 The Notting Hillbillies, including Mark Knopfler, also played at the Albert Halls, in aid of the Dunblane No Guns Fund which was set up when a record was made of Bob Dylan's 'Knockin' on Heaven's Door' which had featured Mark Knopfler. The importance of that record is described later (see Funds).

Forever Young

A note of thanks

Although this publication was undertaken without any expectations of publicity it should be noted that the support of the following turned a dream into reality:

Snap-On-Tools Ltd
Avon Cosmetics Ltd
Rock 'n Bowl (Kettering)
R. Griggs Group Ltd.
C&K Switches Ltd.
Pegasus Group plc.
Johnathan Brown Estate Agents
Kettering Bedding Centre
Kettering Bodycraft
Abbott Property Services
Walls & Floors (Kettering Ltd)

Special thanks to:

Chase Design
John Goddard Design
J. Beattie Accountants
K.C.B.C.
Evening Telegraph
TypeStart Digital Pre-press

Last but not least,
to all those people in
Northamptonshire who took time out of
their lives to write a poem.

This book is dedicated to the
children and their teacher
so tragically killed at
Dunblane Primary School
on March 13th 1996.

———◆———

Forever young was
conceived with tears,
Published with sympathy,
Bought with compassion,
And read, we hope, with joy.

'Forever Young', one of many Books of Poetry, this one from Northamptonshire.

Gifts to the Schools – Dunblane Primary School received many gifts, some like computers, books and benches for the School itself, others to be shared among the pupils. These included Easter eggs, dreamcatchers and soft toys, all of which provided comfort at an especially difficult time for children who had lost siblings or friends and could not comprehend what had happened at their school.

In 1998 the Association of Play Industries donated the Argyle/Braemar Estates Play Park with play equipment for the children of Dunblane.

A Miner's Lamp sent to Dunblane Primary School from Aberfan, a Community which had been left devastated by the Disaster which overtook Pantglas Junior School in October 1966.

11

MEMORIALS

Dunblane Memorial Garden – The Garden was created at Dunblane Cemetery by Stirling Council in the area where 13 of the children and Gwen Mayor are laid to rest. It was made possible through the public's generosity, the cost of developing it met jointly by the Dunblane Fund and the Stirling Observer Dunblane Help Fund (see  Funds). The design incorporated dry stone walls, seating areas, a commemorative plaque and a fountain decorated with coloured pebbles. It was dedicated on the second anniversary of the Tragedy in March 1998. Money from the funds was set aside for continued maintenance of the Garden and is administered by a registered charity, the Dunblane Cemetery Garden Memorial Trust.

The Memorial Garden – (top) Dedication in March 1998 and (l) The Plaque, (r) The Fountain.

Dunblane Primary School – By 2001 a memorial had been placed at the Primary School, incorporating a framed quilt and a plaque donated by Gwen Mayor's family which is hung beside another quilt donated from Lincoln Quilters' Guild, USA. In addition, under a sculpture of a girl with a snowdrop created by Walter Awlson, husband of the School's Assistant Head in 1996, there is a plaque with the wording "Dunblane Primary School staff, pupils and parents, past, present and future will never forget the events of 13 March 1996, and will always remember Class 1/13 and their teachers". A cabinet includes a display of some of the very beautiful and valuable gifts that were donated to the School.

In 2001 a group of bereaved parents placed a cairn, which they designed themselves, in the small garden at the School on the site of the gymnasium where their children died.

Benches, a Sculpture and a Stone – There were gifts of benches, many of which can now be seen around the town, including some in the Memorial Garden. A donated sculpture, 'Friends Forever', sits proudly in a small garden area at the Fourways Roundabout next to Dunblane Sports Club. A stone was placed to the side of the 15th tee at the Dunblane New Golf Club where the golfers have a view across to the Primary School.

Benches - Three of the many donated to Dunblane at the Memorial Garden; A Special Group with Learning Difficulties from Derby who made a Bench incorporating a Heart with the Victims' Names.

Friends Forever – sculpted by William I Sunderland of Atlanta, GA, USA, and donated by the Rotary Clubs of Towsontowne, MD, USA, and Bridge of Allan & Dunblane – Representatives from the US Rotary visited for the Opening Ceremony.

The Marker Stone at the 15th Tee, and the View from Dunblane New Golf Club to the Primary School.

Local Churches – Three local churches commissioned new stained glass windows commemorating Gwen Mayor and her pupils who were represented in the designs. Two of the windows, both gifted by Freemasons, were dedicated in the autumn of 1998. The St Blane's Memorial Window was designed and installed by Roland Mitton and celebrates the release of 'The Spirit'. At Lecropt Kirk the theme is the hymn 'All Things Bright and Beautiful', a window for all children, past, present and future. Its designers were Neil and Bryan Hutchison. At the Holy Family Church three windows were dedicated in February 1999. The initial idea for the windows, 'Lead Kindly Light', was suggested by artist Kenneth King from County Donegal and was interpreted and developed by artist Shona McInnes: the windows were erected by the parishioners of the Church and their friends in Dunblane and beyond.

For Dunblane Cathedral a standing stone of Clashach sandstone was commissioned. The memorial was sculpted and inscribed by Richard Kindersley who describes how "it is carved on all four sides with texts especially chosen for their relevance to the Tragedy and to children, who were the main victims of this brutal act". It was dedicated on 12 March 2000.

Stained Glass Windows at (clockwise from top left) St Blane's Church, the Church of the Holy Family and Lecropt Kirk and (bottom left) the Standing Stone at Dunblane Cathedral.
(Photos from St Blane's and Lecropt: Brother John M Mackay)

Stirling Castle – An altar cover being embroidered by the Stirling Embroiderers' Guild in 1996 had seventeen stars incorporated into its design in memory of the sixteen children and their teacher during its completion. A charity Christmas card depicting the cover was produced to raise funds for Children's Hospice Association Scotland (CHAS).

Altar Cover commissioned for the Chapel Royal at Stirling Castle by Historic Scotland and designed by Malcolm Lochhead of Glasgow Caledonian University – Seventeen Stars were added to the Design after Dunblane. (Photo: Stuart Menelaws)

Tributes at other Schools – We know that many schools, deeply affected by what had happened to fellow pupils and teachers in a small Scottish town, were moved to undertake projects in memory of the Dunblane victims. Gardens were created, trees planted and memorials made. We include pictures of two of them here.

Schools Remember – (l) A Cairn at Carbost Primary School, Isle of Skye, dedicated on 1 May 1997; (r) a Dedication Ceremony at Eassie Primary School, Angus, when a Plaque was erected by a Tree bearing the Words "The Eassie Tree of Life" inspired by Dunblane Primary School 1996.

Some we knew of through personal connections, such as the tree planted at Inverary Primary School, and others through the media. In 2010 we learnt from a report in the *North Devon Journal* of yet another tribute, this one at Braunton School & Community College, Devon, and so typical of all those others we are sorry not to be able to describe here. In 1996 the School had planted daffodils, and the Principal Mr D Sharratt wrote to me to say "Each spring the daffodils make a wonderful display and are a beautiful reminder to our students and the school community of this very sad event". Sadly we know that some other projects have since fallen victim to newer developments, though not without vigorous protests, and I am sure that everybody whose school worked hard to commemorate our children and teacher will never forget, and that is the best memorial.

Tree Planting – The Families were sent details of other trees planted in memory of their loved ones. Many are growing in Israel, some sponsored from Canada in the Canada Forest, others sponsored from the UK and USA in the Jerusalem Peace Forest and the Children's Forest. A number of native Scottish trees were planted on Holy Island off the coast of Arran by the Holy Island Project. There are oak trees at a site near the village of Edwinstowe, in the heart of Sherwood Forest, and a jacaranda tree planted at an Elementary School in Boynton Beach, Florida, as a living memory to the children and their teacher, organised by a local couple whose daughter attended the school – a local nursery had donated the tree for free.

A Flame for Dunblane – The National Association for Primary Education (NAPE) received £12,000 sent spontaneously from primary schools and individuals in England, and their chair, Chris Davis, commissioned a memorial to remember

Dunblane. Sculptor Walter Bailey created 'The Flame', carved from a single yew, which stands within the Conkers complex at the heart of the National Forest in Leicestershire. The opening ceremony was held in April 1998 in the presence of families from Dunblane, the Assistant Bishop of Leicester, members of NAPE National Council and local schoolchildren from Oakthorpe and Donisthorpe who made paper snowdrops for the occasion. George Robertson, then Secretary of State for Defence and now a patron of the Dunblane Centre, dedicated 'The Flame': "This memorial is a flame, bright among the trees and the flowers which will soon bloom around us – throwing its light on the goodness with which we must illuminate the darkness of the past." The parents were each given a mini 'flame' sculpted from the same yew tree.

'The Flame'
(l) at the Opening Ceremony in April 1998, (r) in 2010 with the National Forest now growing around, (bottom) A Flame for Dunblane – "Remembering Days Shared in Innocence. For All the Love Shared Through the Pain".

Chris Davis wrote a beautiful poem 'Children Forever' especially for the occasion. Walter Bailey continues his links with Dunblane and has been commissioned to make the 'Tree of Life' for The Centre as part of the Tenth Anniversary celebrations (see Chapter 8).

SUPPORT FOR OTHERS

A number of organisations used donations they received to support other projects.

The Gwen Mayor Trust was launched by The Educational Institute of Scotland (EIS) and each year awards monies to primary school projects connected with subject areas she loved: the arts, culture, music and sport. Funds were initially raised from teachers in Scottish schools and the Trust has since received money from trade unions and individuals. Among the trustees are one of Gwen Mayor's daughters and a former colleague. In 2012/13 a total of £4,500 was awarded for thirteen projects including the purchase of Wellington boots for an outdoor learning project involving the creation of a 'Garden for Growing' and a regeneration project based on salvaging slates from an old school building to be demolished.

The Graduates' Association at the University of Stirling, where I'd spent my own career, set up a Dunblane Primary School Fund and raised around £6,000 for charity. Their first donation was to Children's Hospice Association Scotland (CHAS).

And having been the recipients of so much generosity ourselves, many of us were determined that whenever possible we too would support projects to raise money and awareness in order to help others, especially children.

Books – The proceeds from the sale of two books about the events in Dunblane supported causes close to our hearts. 'Dunblane: Our Year of Tears', published in 1997 and edited by Peter Samson and Alan Crow, two journalists from the *Sunday Mail*, was a compilation of personal stories from twelve people affected by the Tragedy – its profits supported Save the Children. Mick North's own account 'Dunblane: Never Forget' was published in 2000 and raised money for CHAS and Breakthrough Breast Cancer. Some of its profits also went to the Gun Control Network.

Charity Roses – With the support of the Dunblane Fund two roses, developed by Alec Cocker of James Cocker and Sons, Aberdeen, were named after the Dunblane

Dunblane Roses: (l) Gwen Mayor, (centre) Rod Mayor and Pam Ross at the Rose Planting in Dunblane, (r) Innocence.

victims. They were chosen to complement one another, and sales of 'Gwen Mayor', a Hybrid T rose, have supported the Gwen Mayor Trust while those of 'Innocence', a bushy patio rose chosen by the bereaved parents and named for the children, support CHAS. In August 1997 there was a short ceremony to name the two roses which were planted at the roundabout in Dunblane High Street.

Dunblane Ribbon – At the October 1996 Memorial Service the Families wore tartan ribbons. Afterwards the chair of the Scottish School Boards Association, Ann Hill, suggested the idea that we might use the ribbons in a campaign to support Save the Children. Just under a year later the campaign was launched with ribbons sold in schools throughout Scotland.

In all the Ribbon Campaign income was approximately £300,000. Proceeds for Save the Children from 'Dunblane: Our Year of Tears' had amounted to £30,000, and the charity also received more than a third of a million pounds from the sale of the Dunblane Single (see No Guns Fund). To celebrate the contribution made by the Dunblane families a group of us were invited to a Save the Children reception hosted by their patron, the Princess Royal, on the Royal Yacht Britannia.

*Dunblane Ribbon Campaign
for Save the Children:
(l) Mick North with Aberdeenshire
Primary School Children;*
(Photo: Daily Record)
*(r) Pam Ross and Daughter Alison
(bottom) Dunblane Parents
at a Reception hosted by
The Princess Royal.*

No Guns Fund – The Families were never in any doubt, as was most of the British population, that it was imperative to do everything possible to eliminate the risk of another Dunblane. Against vigorous opposition but with the support of many politicians and the media, they and their friends, especially those in the Snowdrop Campaign and Gun Control Network, helped bring about a change to Britain's gun laws which resulted in the outlawing of handguns. Great Britain now has one of the lowest rates of gun homicide worldwide.

During the autumn of 1996 local musician Ted Christopher approached the parents with a proposal to record a version of 'Knockin' on Heavens Door' with some additional words. It was to be a protest song, its aim to boost the campaign for outlawing handguns, but the record would also raise money for charity. The single was recorded at Abbey Road Studios in London and featured a Mark Knopfler guitar solo and the voices of children from Dunblane, some of whom had lost siblings in March. The recording was followed closely by the media (see http://www.bannockburnband.co.uk/video2.htm for Sky News coverage). The song reached number one in the singles charts and raised a significant amount of money. Additional money came from the Notting Hillbillies' concert in Stirling in May 1997. Almost £500,000 was presented to representatives of Save the Children, Childline and CHAS at an event held at Dunblane Hydro in June 1997. When the Dunblane Centre opened, the No Guns Fund financed the purchase of equipment for the Music Studio (see Chapter 5).

Sleeve from the Dunblane Single, signed by some Dunblane Children who sang on the Record – the Clown Drawing is by Emma Crozier who died on 13 March 1996.

Helping the Victims of Other Tragedies – Over the years many of those who were involved during the Dunblane tragedy have been able to offer advice to others caught up in disasters across the globe. This has been at an official and professional level, involving the clergy, the local authority and medical and mental health staff and, probably most significantly, at a personal level. Since March 1996 too many multiple shootings have taken place across the world and each one has been followed by messages of sympathy and offers of support from Dunblane. The Families themselves have reached out and met with other families struggling to come to terms with what had happened to them, especially at Port

Arthur in Tasmania, Columbine and Sandy Hook in the USA and Winnenden in Germany. Out of the darkness of similar losses have come strong bonds of friendship and support.

Candles lit at the Dunblane Centre for the Victims who died at Sandy Hook Elementary School, CT, on the First Anniversary in December 2013 – see mysandyhookfamily.org

THE FUNDS

Many people and organisations decided that their preferred way to respond to the events at Dunblane was to send money. A few days after the shootings an advisor, who had been invited to a meeting in the Holy Family Church Hall in Dunblane, chaired by the local Director of Education Gordon Jeyes, informed the invited groups, including representatives from the Primary School, head teachers and School Board and PTA members, that money was likely to flood into the town and if this wasn't managed properly it could cause divisions as it had after previous disasters elsewhere. Nora remembers that it was a chilling meeting as nobody was able to process what had happened and the talk of thousands of pounds just seemed irrelevant. Over the next few months some people may have had this warning too much on their minds as concerns with money became over-exaggerated, overly reported and out of proportion. For some time it appeared that gifts intended to help Dunblane were often being viewed as a problem.

Most people sent their donations to the town, the School, one of the local churches, the local authority or, once they were set up, to one of the established funds. A few attempted to make direct contact with the Families – we remember very fondly how representatives of Humberside Fire Brigade came to see us after they had raised £22,000. We were able to put some of this generous donation towards social activities, including our first outing together away from Dunblane – the Eagles' concert at Murrayfield Stadium provided some light relief from the difficult things that had consumed our lives until then. But because of the volume of donations it was not possible to acknowledge all of them or necessarily know every donor's exact wishes. It was perhaps not surprising that, as various groups of people sought to help, a number of independent funds emerged, each trying to do their best. But this multiplicity inevitably led to confusion for the donors and consequent divided loyalties and purposes for the funds. However, it is to the credit of the town that, not without these initial difficulties, it did find a way to handle the money that has since matched the wishes of most of those concerned and has provided lasting legacies.

The main funds that benefited from public donations were:

The Bereaved Families Fund (Dunblane) was a short-lived fund set up within Dunblane which provided immediate help of food and money to the families directly affected. They had set out three simple objectives: to provide immediate relief in support of the existing authorities i.e. pre-cooked meals, transport etc., to help with household bills, and to be able to offer a respite holiday in the course of time. At a time when many family members needed time off work this immediate support was critical. By the time it closed in June 1996 the fund had received over £250,000 and had fulfilled the first two of these objectives. Any further receipts were to be added to the Dunblane Fund.

The Holy Family Church, like many institutions in Dunblane, was the recipient of thousands of messages, which in their case included Mass cards, letters, poems, holy objects and assurances of prayers for the victims and their families. Generous sums of money were also received, including a contribution from the R.C. Diocese of Dunkeld, which were shared among the Families.

Dunblane Primary School Board/PTA Fund was made up of donations sent directly to the Primary School and was maintained as a separate fund. The money was eventually used to fulfil the three most popular suggestions from a public survey of the parents and guardians of all children on the school roll at 13 March. A portion of the fund was split up amongst Dunblane Primary School, Newton Primary School and Dunblane High School to be used at the discretion of the headteachers and their staff, a donation was made to the Gwen Mayor Trust, and a non-charitable trust fund was established with the remaining money and administered for the future needs of the children and the schools.

A number of newspapers had also set up funds. There was a Daily Record Dunblane Donation Fund and the *Sun* also had an appeal which was used for a children's play area at Stirling Royal Infirmary and paid for a trip for some of the Families to Santa Claus Village in Lapland. However, the largest of the funds was set up by the local newspaper, the *Stirling Observer.*

The Stirling Observer Dunblane Help Fund was a charitable trust and received donations that reached £2,032,700. Its trustees were David Howarth, Alexander Cargill, Anita Dufton, Pat Greenhill and Marjorie Davies. Although its purposes were similar to those of the Dunblane Fund (see below), its charitable status placed limits on what it could do, in particular with respect to direct assistance to the Families. The trustees could provide financial help to try to relieve distress and suffering of those affected and also support any charitable purposes which they considered to be of help to the community of Dunblane in the light of the Tragedy. In accordance with the second purpose there was agreement that some kind of permanent memorial would be appropriate along with financial assistance for individual memorials such as headstones.

The fund's first communication was unfortunately timed. In April 1996 a questionnaire 'Your View' was circulated throughout Dunblane, asking residents to rank in order of preference which of the following ventures they felt would be the most appropriate use of the fund. These were a Community Centre/Sports Centre, a Swimming Pool, a Memorial Garden, the money to be split between the Community and the families of the bereaved and injured and the money equally divided between the families of the bereaved and injured. Many residents opted for the Swimming Pool. However, plenty of others, including the Families, considered the questionnaire premature, being circulated as it was within weeks of the shootings. A number of people spoke out, saying that no decision on a community project should be taken so soon after the event. It was suggested that a period of time would be needed before the Families should be asked to express views on the further uses to which the funds might be put. In the meantime the fund paid for headstones for the victims and ensured that some money was received by the Families.

The Dunblane Fund was set up by the local authority. Initially administered by interim trustees, within months permanent independent trustees were appointed, namely Lieutenant Colonel James Stirling of Garden (Chair), Sheriff Robert Younger (Vice-Chair), Councillor Pat Kelly (Stirling Council), Ian Ross (former Director of Social Work for Central Regional Council) and Pat Greenhill (former Provost of Stirling District Council). Bob Jack and Bill Dickson from Stirling Council were appointed as secretary and treasurer, respectively and KPMG, Chartered Accountants, as auditors whose services were offered at no cost to the fund.

In addition to the individual donations a number of high profile activities and events also raised money. These included all the proceeds from the sale of 'Purple Heather', recorded by Rod Stewart with the Scotland Squad for football's Euro '96, and those from the concert given by Chris de Burgh at Stirling Castle in July 1996. The fund also received money from the Dunblane International, hosted by the Scottish Rugby Union at Murrayfield in August 1996, when Scotland's rugby squad played a match against the Barbarians in a tribute to the local community. Money received by the Stirling firm of Whyler Photos, who had taken the class photograph and been paid for this by the *Daily Record,* was also passed onto the Dunblane Fund.

The fund's purposes had been set out at length in a trust deed and described, briefly, in 'A Message from the Trustees' issued in July 1996:
- The primary purpose of the fund is to make provision for the relief of loss suffered by those affected by the Tragedy
- After this, the main subsidiary purpose of the trust are to make provision for a suitable memorial for those killed in the Tragedy and to make provision for the benefit of the community of Dunblane (although initially in March the focus appeared to be entirely on those directly affected by the Tragedy)

The fund provided immediate payment to the Families to help with funeral expenses and this was followed by further payments. It received its last donations on 31 March 1997 and any money received after that date was given to the Stirling Observer Fund for the purpose of benefiting the community of Dunblane. The total donations had risen to £5,248,000 by the time it closed.

A fund agent was appointed who provided a confidential link between the Families and the trustees, and he also liaised with the Stirling Observer Fund with whom close cooperation was promised. They shared a trustee, coordinated some of their activities and were jointly responsible for funding the development of the Memorial Garden. This set the pattern for supporting a community project.

Dunblane Community Trust – In March 1998 approximately £800,000 and £1,300,000 remained in the Dunblane Fund and the Stirling Observer Fund, respectively. The funds took information from a Stirling Observer Community Survey on the current status of community proposals. By May 1999 a new Dunblane Community Trust (DCT) came into existence and was given charitable status, and the money in the other funds was paid over to it. In a letter of 16 July 1999 from Pat Greenhill, the Families were told that the aim of DCT would be to provide funding for the Dunblane Youth Project Trust, to assist in its creation of a new Youth Centre for Dunblane on the former TA Hall site at Duckburn. As the following chapters reveal, this proved to be a very significant step in the story of the Dunblane Centre.

Postscript

Here's a Glaswegian tale from **Gordon Brown**, who in 1996 was General Manager for the Carnegies Leisure Group, the largest licence trade operators in Scotland, and manager of the Bonkers Showbar in Glasgow. It encapsulates so much of the heartfelt support which countless people wanted to give to Dunblane.

"Everything happened just a few days after the tragic event .... what was to unfold was special beyond belief.

"Through my job I knew lots of footballers and, as we called them at the time, pop stars, so the first thing I done was call on the services of Wet Wet Wet and the next thing, a selection of gold discs arrived to auction off at a 'Charity Night for Dunblane'. What a start I thought! I discussed with colleagues the possibility of everyone doing something similar with their contacts so that we could have a live auction on the night of the 'do'. I must admit I was met with "I don't know pop stars or footballers", but they all said they would try their best to get someone to donate something. Being an optimist I set my heart on raising £2,000, which I thought was entirely achievable.

"Big ask, but I thought we could do it. At Bonkers, we got together and made a plan!!! One of the guys who had a reputation for telling stories duly said, "My pal is Neil (Doctor) Fox from TV and radio"...........to whit the others said "Aye, right!" He said, "I'll give him a shout". Anyway, we all thought up ways of involving anyone and everyone. All business folk in Glasgow and surrounding areas became interested in getting involved. The rolling stone gathered momentum very, very quickly and all the guys tried to outdo each other with who they could get involved and what they could get them to donate: from

the owners of Albion Rovers donating a garden shed to Daniel O'Donnell sending gold discs from the Emerald Isle. Then a box arrived from London with a leather biker's jacket signed with a 'squiggle', which turned out to be Mark Knopfler from Dire Straits!! Meat Loaf, Glasgow Rangers, Glasgow Celtic all followed that morning and I thought, this is getting ridiculous. A flurry of stuff came, everything from free haircuts and fish and chips for a year, back stage passes for every concert under the sun, season tickets, World Cup signed strips, free travel, holidays, meals for two and even free rolls and sausage! The list was truly endless. Another guy said "I've got a signed football from the Lisbon Lions which is burst and lying underneath ma wean's cot. Any Guid!?!"

"The night drew closer and we had all the Radio Clyde guys and Tom Ferrie from the BBC to conduct the auction. Footballers, models and the odd celebrity were calling to see if they could get in! On the night bidding was ferocious and it turned out a huge success. We ended up raising upwards of twenty grand. The people of Glasgow, the business folk and indeed the Bonkers' clientele, excelled their selves, and I am so proud that what started as a wee idea, ended in a fantastic effort from all concerned. There is never a moment when I don't think about 'That Fantastic Night' and what the wee folk can do! Mine and everyone's thoughts are always with the families and folk of Dunblane."

CHAPTER 3 – WHERE IT ALL BEGAN

NORA GILFILLAN
with contributions from STAN BRADLEY, LES MORTON, ELEANOR BRAILSFORD and ALAN ROBINSON

MARCH 1996

The Dunblane Community was in a state of sadness, shock and disbelief. People felt stunned, unable to take in the enormity of the horrific tragedy at our school. I remember a sense of being cold for days with a heavy feeling of despair deep inside. I recall thinking that if I feel like this, it must be unbearable for the families who had lost children and the others whose children were injured. There were also the many people who had tried to help and witnessed scenes too unbearable to describe. Compared to these people I was unaffected, yet I did feel deeply affected. I know many others who felt the same.

The Tragedy had also touched people far beyond Dunblane, and people from all over the world wanted to show kindness and their sympathy. In Chapter 2 we have remembered the many gifts and donations that came to Dunblane. At the time I was only aware of the gifts sent to the Community as a whole which had a great impact on Dunblane. Before the children's funerals and the reopening of the School, I recall how many volunteers helped move the thousands of bouquets of flowers which had been laid along the streets outside the school entrance and transfer them to Dunblane Cemetery. They were carefully laid in rows so that the messages of sympathy were displayed. It seemed so unreal seeing all the bright colours of so many beautiful flowers. Many have commented on the silence but for the gentle rustle of the cellophane wrappers fluttering in the breeze – these flowers represented the kindness of so many people who just wanted to show they cared. Hundreds of gifted teddy bears and soft toys were displayed in St Blane's Hall and subsequently every child in Dunblane got to choose one of these to keep.

Various community leaders became involved in diverse projects. A vacant shop in the High Street (now Mary's Meals) was opened as the Drop-In Centre, manned by local volunteers, where seating was provided and cups of tea offered and the thousands of cards and letters of sympathy sent to the town were displayed. Gifts and offers of help and support from all over the world continued to pour into Dunblane. I was only aware of a fraction of what arrived, but I do know there were dreamcatchers and angel brooches gifted to every one of the more than 700 children in the Primary School. I knew about the money – cash and lots of cheques from every corner of the globe. There were also gifts of the people themselves and their time, talents and skills, ranging from puppet shows to free Shen sessions. A small group of parents from the two other P1 classes at the Primary School obtained the lists of offers from our local council and organised a range of activities over the summer holidays in 1996. It was successful and helped bring the parents and the young children together. In the days, weeks and months following the Tragedy the Community struggled to come to terms with what had happened. Experts were sent in to provide support – I remember the Braeport Centre (the site of the old primary school) was set up with social workers on call and the Community were encouraged to seek support.

There remained, however, one group which was sidelined - the older children, teenagers and young adults. Dunblane did not have any informal youth groups. There were, and still are, very well organised uniform groups, including the Boys' Brigade, Girl Guides and Air Cadets, but if young people wanted to hang out together their only option was to meet on street corners or at the play parks. Small groups of teenagers, some of whom were relatives of the victims, would get together and chat in the Drop-In Centre in the High Street, but this was not suitable and indeed some of the adults felt it was not 'right' that they were hanging around. Stan Bradley, a local resident and policeman, was made aware of the 'problem'. Stan had been a volunteer with youth clubs in Dunblane since 1978 and had previously started a 'Friday night club' as a youth drop-in facility, a venture which had begun to peter out by early 1996. He spoke to some of those who had been asked to move on and recognised that the 'problem' was the lack of provision for these youngsters. They needed somewhere of their own where they could grieve and share their feelings with each other, in their own way.

Here in **Stan Bradley's** own words is what happened next:

"The youngsters left the Drop-In Centre and headed down to their usual haunts. After talking to the volunteers I went and spoke to the youngsters, all of whom were known to me personally. I engaged them in conversation about the purpose of the High Street Centre and the reason for its existence. They told me they had started to use it because of all the media and public presence in Dunblane town centre and that they just wanted to be out of the way.

Aerial View of the TA Buildings as they were in January 1999.

"I asked them whether it would be a help if they had a place to go and they almost bit my hand off. Knowing that the old Territorial Army (TA) training centre was not being used I contacted the relevant authority and made enquiries with a view to getting it for a drop-in facility for the kids. The TA granted us the use of the building cost free but on the condition that we would vacate the premises when they were to be sold in the near future. I posted a notice in the High Street Drop-In Centre to see if I could get some volunteers to give me a hand with setting up such a venture. The response was overwhelming, and without the dedication and enthusiasm of those volunteers this project would have gone no further.

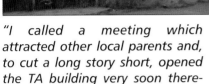

"I called a meeting which attracted other local parents and, to cut a long story short, opened the TA building very soon there-after. Because of the goodwill shown I managed to 'scrounge' some youth club equipment and foodstuffs for a tuck shop. The facility was an immediate success in terms that 60–80 youngsters attended each evening from Monday to Thursday. I have to say that everybody, adults and youngsters alike, quickly bonded into a 'family' group.

"I ran the Youth Drop-in for a good few weeks until it was necessary to devolve some of the associated duties such as general administration and book-keeping. After a period of some weeks the volunteers and youngsters gained mutual familiarity and respect and volunteers were able to identify with each individual's specific traits and problems. Various activities were run for those that came along, including discos, arts and crafts nights, music and even soup making, as some of the adults there felt there was a need for this. There were also away trips organised.

Soon the Youth Drop-in became a home from home for the youngsters

"It wasn't all a bed of roses. Youngsters being young-sters, there were a few occasions when some of them were more than boisterous and caused problems at The Drop-in to a point where some volunteer helpers found it more than they could handle. This resulted in 'natural wastage', as it were, and new helpers were sought to replace those who moved on. But this in no way detracted from the assistance and commitment of the volunteers at that early stage and, indeed, throughout the ensuing period.

Stan Bradley.

"On one occasion during the summer of 1996 I was at home having a night away from The Drop-in, when I received a frantic telephone call from one of the volunteers during which, in the background, I could hear 'World War III' starting! I went straight down to The Drop-in but on arrival when I entered the building, I could have heard a pin drop. Without exception all the youths were on their best behaviour; however, the volunteers were on their last legs!

27

"On a sadder note, there were two occasions during that summer when the Youth Drop-in was needed to help the youngsters through further bereavements which had a huge impact on all the regulars. It was opened for the youngsters to come along with their pals and get some comfort in familiar surroundings, and if nothing else these youths responded with great humility and respect"

Stan's commitment had gone beyond his uniform. Within days, news of the venture had got out the old fashioned way, by word of mouth – this was before the days of social media and the now ubiquitous mobile phone. Nearly two decades on young people would no doubt use their mobile phones or Facebook to support and talk to one another, but in the mid-nineties they had to meet together. The Youth Drop-in was a great success and it became apparent to Stan that a permanent facility was needed.

APRIL 1997

Stan Bradley describes how:

"In April 1997 I was advised by the Territorial Army that the sale of the premises was imminent. As The Drop-in had been such a success I felt this would be a huge loss, not only to the youngsters, but to the wider community if we could not continue to operate. In light of this, I had a thought that if we could somehow secure the premises in our favour, then we could maybe formalise the situation and perhaps apply to other sources, such as the National Lottery, and create a permanent facility."

Stan approached the Stirling Observer Dunblane Help Fund (see Chapter 2) and asked them to purchase the building for the drop-in group. They agreed and the purchase was completed in November 1997. Stan was delighted – it was a big step to ensuring a permanent centre. The young people loved having somewhere to hang out, but the building was in a terrible state and volunteers will remember the frost inside the building, and the birds inside the roof, which leaked. It would only be a matter of time before it was no longer suitable as a venue.

Stan recalls arranging a meeting around this time:

"I called a meeting of all the volunteers, and presented my thoughts to them. Although everyone was sympathetic to that cause, at this point the volunteer helpers, in the main, felt that we had, perhaps, run our course and they did not want to become part of anything more formal. However, Alan Robinson approached me after the meeting and said that he thought it was a good idea and he would become involved. I contacted relevant organisations in Dunblane in a bid to get responsible people together to set the ball in motion. This then was the conception of what we have today."

Stan expressed his hopes for renovating or even building a new 'youth drop-in centre' on the site and said they needed to find ways to fundraise. He felt that with the support of Alan, who was a trained youth worker and local resident and had been volunteering in the Youth Drop-in since the early days, they could move the project forward. They started to make plans on how they could get more people involved. They knew that they would need local support and, using whatever contacts they had, approached many local people including church representatives, business people, community groups, the schools and the bereaved and injured family groups. Alan phoned and invited me along to a meeting about the Youth Drop-in and to learn about their plans. He did not go into a lot of detail, but I was immediately interested. From memory about 30 people were there that first evening. I recognised most of them, Dunblane is like that, a town where you knew most people at least by sight. Stan made an impassioned presentation of what had been happening in The Drop-in and his hopes for the future. Everybody was very supportive of Stan and Alan's vision for a permanent building for the

(l) Dunblane Youth Centre Volunteers: (back row) Gordon Mann, Catriona Whitton, Eleanor Brailsford, Margo Baxter, Maureen Simpson, Catherine McKay, (front row) Izzy Greig, Linda McGhee, Kathy Crockett in the temporary Youth Club unit in Duckburn Estate; (r) Nicky Lewis, the Captain of Dunblane New Golf Club, presenting a Minibus for the Dunblane Youth Centre to Laura McGhee.

young people. Not everybody felt they were able to make the type of commitment that would be necessary to move the project forward, but a steering committee did arise from this meeting and we arranged to meet again the following Sunday. During the early days there were about 12 regular attendees though the number did decrease as the years went on.

Meanwhile the Youth Drop-in continued to thrive and there was a good core of local adult volunteers who worked tirelessly to ensure the facility continued. Stan had been right, there was a clear need for a youth facility.

Eleanor Brailsford recalls an important role for the Youth Drop-In:

"Towards the end of 1995 I had heard of the appalling aftermath of the nuclear reactor disaster in Chernobyl which happened in April 1986 and how people in the UK were helping the children affected by this by offering a month's respite

in their own homes. I contacted some friends and their families in Dunblane, and we realised this was something we could and would enjoy organising.

"We spent many months fundraising and organising events, but just as we were confirming arrangements for this exciting visit the dreadful event that changed Dunblane forever happened at Dunblane Primary. It was impossible to think beyond the children who were killed, their families and of course our own children. At this time the visit from the children from Chernobyl was obviously delayed, perhaps never to happen. We just did not discuss it as we dealt with the shock of a tragedy of our own. But by the beginning of 1997 we finally began to get ready and were, and continued to be, proud of the generosity of the whole community of Dunblane and how they made the visit, which did eventually take place in June 1997, so very special for ten very lucky children from Belarus.

"We needed a 'hub' to meet, drop off and pick up the children and share the care of these visitors, and I approached Stan and Alan to ask if the Youth Drop-in could be used for this. In a short time, we had access to The Drop-in, the Community had donated toys, videos, lunches, clothes – the list was endless and The Drop-in was perfect. Previously, we had nowhere like it in Dunblane and it was lovely to see the young people of Dunblane and the children from Belarus playing together in a space that we had no idea would become the hub of our community."

After discussions it was agreed that the only way forward for the Youth Project would be to have a brand new building. So the next step was to get an idea of what sort of building we could have on the site. A local architect was invited along to one of our meetings and he discussed what would be possible. It was thought that we would need about £200,000 for a purpose-built youth centre. It would not be dissimilar to the present TA building in that it would have a tuck shop, a drop-in area with pool tables, TVs and sofas and a larger area suitable for discos and a platform for bands. Although we were aware that there were funds earmarked for community use, at this stage we never assumed that we would be offered any. After all, the Stirling Observer Fund had already paid for the site, and we were aware that there were ongoing discussions in Dunblane about other projects such as improving the existing Victoria Hall, a venue used by the wider community. We could not necessarily expect to be given any more funds.

Then quite out of the blue, at least to me, our local councillor Pat Greenhill, who was a trustee of the Dunblane Fund and chair of the Stirling Observer Fund, came along to one of our Sunday night meetings and presented us with an important proposition. If our committee was willing to build something much bigger than a drop-in youth centre, something which included a sports hall facility that would be open to the whole community, money remaining in the funds could be used to support the entire project. This raised a dilemma for the committee. Although the offer would solve our funding problem it would change the original aims for the project into something significantly bigger. It was emphasised that we would have to be solely responsible for the running of the proposed new centre and there would be no additional financial support from the local authority, Stirling Council. Over the next seven years we were reminded many times that we would be given only the capital funding and it would be entirely up to us to generate the revenue. Further discussion was necessary. Obviously no matter how keen we were to have funding for the youth centre, the reality of being responsible for a larger and much more expensive project was daunting, to say the least. However, despite some reservations we decided unanimously to take up the challenge.

NOVEMBER 1997

Our group needed to be formalised. Douglas Whyte, a local solicitor, was enlisted, and a constitution drawn up. The Dunblane Youth Project Trust was officially formed in November 1997 and later became the Dunblane Youth and Sports Centre Trust (DY&SCT) – I remember we wanted to ensure that 'Youth' was prominent in the name as we felt strongly that we did not want the whole project hijacked by the wider community with the result that the young people were sidelined yet again. Its founding trustees were Stan Bradley (appointed its first Chairman), Alan Robinson (Vice-Chairman), Les Morton (Treasurer), David Walsh, David Chisholm, Alan Booth and Nora Dougherty [Gilfillan]. When Stan and David Walsh later resigned, Rog Jefferies and Jim Cattan became trustees. Alan took over as chairman and Nora was later appointed as project co-ordinator. The other trustees had specific skills and contacts that would prove useful over the coming years, but the most important qualities that everyone had were commitment, determination and enthusiasm.

The trust met every Sunday in the old TA building. Now with potential funding available we needed formally to appoint an architect. Three local firms, Robertsons, Harley and Murray and WB_arc, submitted presentations of their vision of the type of building we could have. All of them stated that, whilst it was a good site, the slope and tight space available made it difficult for the full-sized sports hall. They brought varying ideas and plans, all showing in different styles how to make good use of the site. I remember Willie Brown (WB_arc) brought along a 'mock up' of The Centre, and it was definitely helpful to see what the

 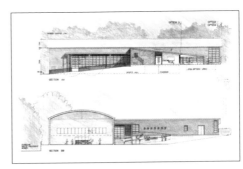

Plans for the Centre: WB_arc's Mock up, Day Sketch. (Images: WB_arc)

31

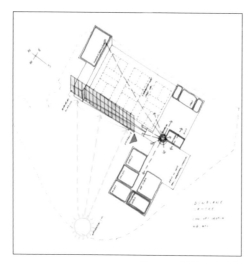

Concept Sketch, Floor Plan. (Images: WB_arc)

actual building could look like. Subsequently Willie Brown was engaged as our architect, with Gordon Pomphrey as the structural engineer and Frank Carroll the quantity surveyor. They must have been frustrated with us at various times over the next few years, trying to communicate with a committee from whom it proved almost impossible to get a consensus of opinion at times. However, their commitment to the cause was unquestioned and their work invaluable.

MARCH 1998

In March 1998, the group sent out a questionnaire to the wider community to try and gauge the support for the project. Concerns were raised about the site and its suitability, especially in relation to road safety, as The Centre was to sit beside a dual carriageway and access was poor. However, the general consensus was that it was a good site for 'noisy' activities. As always in Dunblane, the most popular request was for the project to include a swimming pool. But this could never be a serious consideration. Whilst the construction of a swimming pool would not have been particularly costly, we learned very quickly when researching for our business plan that the cost of running one would be high and therefore outside the budget. Sixteen years later the lack of a publicly-funded swimming pool in Dunblane remains a contentious issue, especially as the new Dunblane High School is the only local secondary school which has not been provided with one.

In the meantime the money left in the Stirling Observer Dunblane Help Fund and the Dunblane Fund was to be administered by a new charity, the Dunblane Community Trust (DCT, see Chapter 2). A working relationship had to be established between Dunblane Youth & Sports Centre Trust (DY&SCT), now also a registered charity, and DCT. Demarcation lines were set up:

- DY&SCT to be responsible for building design, business plan, management and running of the new Centre
- DCT to be responsible for review and approval of all plans and, of course, funding all approved expenditure

Stirling Council provided secretarial and legal services to DCT. What was repeatedly made crystal clear from the outset was that there would be zero financial assistance from the Council for this project. Whatever the outcome, whatever was built, whatever problems ensued – these were to be the responsibility of DY&SCT alone. Stirling Council's stance was no doubt influenced by its recent bailout of the McLaren Centre in Callander which had experienced severe financial difficulties and would, without council support, have gone bust. The Dunblane project was going to be quite an undertaking for a bunch of volunteers!

Alan Robinson later remarked:

"If we had known that it would take us six years to finish – that we would be building a new roundabout, that we would have to raise another £200,000 ourselves, that we would have to keep a youth club going four nights a week while we did it – and that we would give up our Sunday nights for the foreseeable future – I doubt that there would have been any takers"

Nevertheless, the challenge to create a youth and sports facility, managed by local volunteers and funded by the donations received, was taken on. We set off on a journey which, despite our inexperienced team and with no operating 'safety net', did lead to the creation of a unique building and a unique facility.

CHAPTER 4 –
PLANNING AND BUILDING THE DUNBLANE CENTRE

LES MORTON
with contributions from NORA GILFILLAN, ALAN DAVIDSON, WILLIE BROWN, ELEANOR BRAILSFORD and MAUREEN SIMPSON

LES MORTON WAS THE DUNBLANE YOUTH AND SPORTS CENTRE TRUST'S
FOUNDING TREASURER AND FATHER OF EMILY, ONE OF THE DUNBLANE
VICTIMS

1997 TO 2003 - SETBACKS, PROBLEMS & DELAYS

How long does it take to design and build a facility when the funding is in place
and you have a dedicated team of volunteers and professionals? Answer – a lot
longer than you might think or expect!!

THE CAPITAL BUDGET

Despite cordial relations between the Dunblane Youth and Sports Centre Trust
(DY&SCT) and the Dunblane Community Trust (DCT) we immediately had a
significant problem. DCT wanted to know what we were planning to build.
DY&SCT wanted to know how much money was available. Our architect Willie
Brown stated the obvious – how could he design a building without knowing his
budget? This issue went round in circles for months with suggestions ranging
from £800,000 up to £1,600,000.
  We constantly stated that we wanted to build the best possible facility with the
money available, we just did not know exactly how much there was and didn't
want Willie to be wasting time and money designing buildings that had no chance
of being approved. Not being in charge of the money and, indeed, not knowing
how much was available was a big problem for DY&SCT.
  The actual building eventually cost precisely £1,613,412.37, but with
professional fees, fixtures & fittings and other costs the final spend exceeded
£2,000,000.

GRUMBLINGS IN THE COMMUNITY

When it was publicised that the project was going ahead there were many in the
Community who were aggrieved that Stirling Council was getting 'off the hook'.
It was well known that council spending for Dunblane was not a priority and this
caused agitation in a number of people who questioned why donations following
the Tragedy were being used to fund facilities that should properly be supplied by
the Council. With justification, local people also wanted details of what we were
planning to build, but for a while these plans were sketchy at best and this too
caused some unrest.

THE 'RANSOM STRIP'

Dunblane Community Trust (DCT) now owned the land purchased by The Stirling Observer Dunblane Help Fund on which The Centre was to be built (see Chapters 2 and 3), but unfortunately the grassy perimeter was not part of the property originally bought and was under different ownership. Although it looked quite a small piece of land, its acquisition would increase the site by a third and provide just about enough land for the legally-required minimum parking spaces for the building. Even with this extra piece of land the site was described as 'tight' by our architect, Willie Brown, because of its size, shape and slope. So with the help of Douglas Whyte, our solicitor and company secretary, we eventually discovered ownership in Hong Kong. A sum of £18,000 disappeared form our funds for its purchase.

CUSTOMS & EXCISE – enter the dreaded VAT man

It had never occurred to us that we would have to pay VAT on the building expenditure. The funding for the project was donated literally by thousands of individuals and organisations from all over the world. Why should Chancellor Gordon Brown get a boost to his finances because of a tragedy?

However, after researching the VAT legislation (undoubtedly the worst task faced by the treasurer during the entire process) it was clear that specialist advice and interpretation of tax law was required. We entered into discussions and communications with Her Majesty's Customs and Excise, putting forward our case as to why we should not be liable for VAT.

Whilst Customs and Excise were sympathetic to our case and reasoning – even sending a team from London to Scotland to review with us the entire background, funding and plans – after a year we received a letter from Treasury Minister Paul Boateng confirming that we would have to pay VAT on the capital spend. This increased spending on the building by almost £250,000, an absolutely huge amount of money in the circumstances.

Death and taxes, never were truer words spoken!!

Having previously decided that the cost of building the Dunblane Centre would be entirely funded from the worldwide donations received, we now made one single exception because we all felt that the VAT decision, whilst entirely legal, was immoral. We applied for a grant from **sport**scotland and were awarded £200,000 for a Sports Development Programme. This award greatly eased the financial pain of the VAT decision.

ENTRY & EXIT – a new road system

Because the site was bordered by the main Stirling Road the issue of safe entry and exit to The Centre became an important discussion point.

Plans were presented to us by Stirling Council showing a new road system which would ensure that we fully complied with Health & Safety Regulations by the construction of a new mini-roundabout at our entry and exit point. This made complete sense to us, but then we were hit with the bombshell news that in order for this new road layout to proceed we would be required to contribute £46,500.

When this became more widely known some people in the Community were outraged, pointing out that Stirling Council

Claredon Roundabout.

had been planning to upgrade Stirling Road for more than a decade and that we should not be 'subsidising' local government from publicly-donated money. But we had no option other than to agree to the upgrade of the road system – no new road, no planning permission – and we kissed goodbye to another large sum.

Planning permission for the new building was granted in June 2001.

TENSIONS & CONFLICTS

It is impossible for a large group of people to work together over a number of years without episodes of tension and conflict. We had our fair share of these. Sometimes progress was so slow that some people wanted to express publicly their disappointment in others. Sometimes weeks would pass with no tangible progress. Sometimes it could feel as if we were going backwards.

Inevitably there were occasional personality clashes as strongly expressed opinions were reined in by the overall group. However, since everyone had a full-time job and was giving up her or his spare time to volunteer for this project there was, in general, a realistic mind-frame about how we were proceeding. Never having attempted anything like this before we just had to grin and bear all the setbacks and disappointments. Sometimes through gritted teeth!

During the time that all this was happening we were running a very popular youth programme which had moved to the adjacent Duckburn Industrial Estate in Autumn 2001. Seeing hundreds of local kids having fun every week was very motivational for the team, many of whom were volunteer supervisors of the youth programmes.

CREATING THE BUSINESS PLAN

In order to gain approval to spend what eventually amounted to over £2,000,000 we required two things (i) a building plan with precise details of exactly what we would build together with precise costs and (ii) a business plan outlining income and expenditure once The Centre was built and demonstrating plainly that it would be self-funding and sustainable.

Clearly, the first requirement would fall on the shoulders of our professional advisors with input from the volunteers. However, if responsibility for running The Centre was to fall to the trustees and volunteers, creating a business plan was not only essential to having the project approved for funding but was a fantastic learning opportunity. We had to educate ourselves about exactly what it was we were going to run.

Equipped only with a rough outline of the activities we wanted to offer, **Nora Dougherty [Gilfillan]** was charged with visiting other facilities. She recalls:

"My task was to acquire information on everything from the variety of activities on offer, pricing structures, customer numbers through to staffing levels and other significant cost areas. Although there were other leisure centres in the area, our building was going to offer much more than either just a youth club or a leisure centre. Along with a number of our youth club volunteers we visited several youth projects, notably the Café Project in Arbroath, the Space Place in Troon and the Peace Centre in Warrington. Colin Parry, whose son Tim was killed in the bombing at Warrington, made us very welcome and gave us a tour of the newly built Peace Centre. These visits were helpful in giving us ideas of what sort of activities we could offer young people but, perhaps even more importantly, boosted the volunteers' morale at a time when the project seemed to be making slow progress. Sheriff Norrie Stein of the Café Project was without doubt the most inspirational advocate for involving local volunteers to work together with young people – we invited him to our Opening Ceremony, one of the very few guests who had no direct link with Dunblane."

"The most useful information for costings was obtained from the McLaren Community Leisure Centre in nearby Callander and the Castlemilk Project in Glasgow, both of which were council-supported facilities but nevertheless gave us an idea of how much we might expect our costs would be. It was a steep learning curve!"

Nora presented the results of her research to the treasurer. After detailed discussion of where she had visited, to whom she'd spoken and what she had learned, the obvious question was "can I see your notes?" Onto the table tumbled dozens of scraps of paper covered in figures, names, issues, memory joggers – in no particular order. Nora insisted somewhere on these scraps of paper was the answer to all and any questions anybody might have, a claim that was never disproved.

Using this 'research' and the outline plan for the building we set about attempting to answer the key questions:

- How much demand would there be for each of our key activities?
- How much should we charge for each activity?
- Should we offer a membership scheme?
- How many staff would we need, full-time and part-time, and what skills were required?

- What contracts did we need (security, equipment maintenance, admin system, etc.)?
- and on, and on, and on……..

The business plan was the financial expression of the answers (guesses and estimates) to the questions we asked ourselves and reality checked against Nora's research. The business plan told the story and outlined the figures of what we hoped to achieve.

What made the plan credible and believable was one crucial statement, which was:

We break-even at 25% capacity usage

In other words, if the facility was generating revenue for only a quarter of the available hours we would not lose money, a crucial factor remembering the repeated warnings from Stirling Council.

Our combined thought on this was that if The Centre were not used to at least 25% capacity then Dunblane did not deserve such a facility. But we had every confidence that it could be a huge success.

Over a period of weeks Willie and his team had been refining and finalising the drawings and costs for the building. In September 2002 he held a consultation meeting with local young people at the Youth Centre. Eventually the Building Design and Business Plan was forwarded to Dunblane Community Trust (DCT) for review. A couple of meetings were held during which we addressed questions raised by DCT, and without much fanfare everything was approved. Now all we had to do was turn our plans into reality.

2003 TO 2004 – BUILDING THE DUNBLANE CENTRE

In July 2003 it was announced in the *Stirling Observer* that work was to begin on the new Centre. The TA Buildings were finally demolished in September and the new build could start. This would be something that could have tested the patience of our neighbours at the Dunblane Bowling Club.

Alan Davidson, Dunblane Bowling Club, recalls:

"The Bowling Club had a good relationship with the contractors especially the site foreman who was very friendly considering the work in front of him. We had coffee in his office and vice versa to the Club. The contractors parked their cars/vans on our ground when needed and off-loaded larger lorries in our car park when necessary."

June 2004 - Three Months till Opening Day

As the building work progressed exactly on schedule we had to turn our attention to the detailed management and running of The Centre:

- When should we recruit staff, most importantly the manager?
- How would we run and supervise the various activities to be offered?
- Who would be the fitness instructors and how would their contracts be structured?
- How would the administration system work?
- What level of marketing/advertising was required?

There were dozens of issues that now required precise solutions rather than general thoughts, and there was one significant black cloud hovering over us at this time – we had no money for working capital. How could we employ a manager for The Centre when we had no funds for a salary? Fortunately we had connections in the Scottish business community who very generously donated adequate funds which enabled us to get over this hurdle. And so we proceeded to interviewing for this crucial post.

We recognised the sensitivity of this position and that this very sensitivity might be a drawback in attracting suitably qualified applicants. Expectations for The Centre would be sky high, maybe unrealistically so. However, Scott Neil was duly appointed. He had been working at a leisure centre in Fife and clearly saw this as a huge opportunity but also realised that this was an extremely challenging under-taking for him.

Following his appointment Scott was invited to the next trustees' meeting. He listened to extensive discussions about all the problems we had, our lack of funds, differing views on solutions to various issues – he must have thought "what on earth have I got myself into here?" Some of the trustees thought he might resign before he had really started. We certainly had more problems than answers at that particular time, however we were slowly but surely working at the detail of what we wanted to put in place. We were discovering that there is a significant difference between having a general plan and actually dealing with the reality and detail of what it was we were trying to put in place.

The devil is in the detail, how true!

However, with Scott in place all the important issues were progressed (see Chapter 5). All the other staff positions were filled without too much trouble and, although activity was constant and frantic, we were in decent shape as Grand Opening Day loomed ever nearer.

Before such a public and high profile event nobody is ever 100% satisfied with the state of preparation. There are always more things to be done – but time runs out and the big day arrives.

The Centre at various Stages of Construction and Fitting Out. (Photos: WB_arc)

THE BRAND NEW CENTRE

Willie Brown and his project team, Catherine Fyfe, Jude Harper and Joanna Carlile, had more than fulfilled the design aims they'd set out:

"Our aim was to design a building that would provide an exciting and inspiring location for the social and physical development of the young people of Dunblane, while affording great respect to all who suffered from the traumatic events of March 1996.

"Sunlight ingress, and views in and out, quickly become important design generations.

"The facilities provided, sports hall, drop-in café, recording studio, stage, disco space, art room, sprung floor gym/dance studio, were chosen as a result of consultation with the young people of Dunblane.

"As the volume of space required to accommodate all of the above is unavoidably large, careful manipulation of levels and slopes already existing on the site was required to ensure that the building had a human scale, and friendly, easily accessible, sheltered entrance. This, coupled with the desire to ensure wheelchair

Inside The Centre (l) The Ramps; (r) The Sports Hall. (Photos: Shannon Tofts)

access to all parts of the building, led to vertical circulation in the major mass, that housing the Sports Hall, being organised around dramatic ramps visible from the outside.

"Horizontal circulation is organised from entry into reception in the crook of an elbow in plan, with sports facilities to the left, accessed from ramps, and all other facilities in the lower lean-to section of the building, leading from noisy disco/stage, through drop-in café, computer suite, art room, to quiet required for recording studio.

41

"As the building has to be economically viable in use, it is important that running costs are kept to a minimum, so low energy systems such as underfloor heating are incorporated, and low maintenance materials such as aluminium roof sheeting, exposed blockwork, walls and steel structure are specified.

"For the same reason, the building is designed to allow for minimum number of staff to run the facility by maximising visual contact/supervision from reception to all the main spaces. This also helps new visitors to orientate themselves, and the large west facing glazing allows natural light to flow through the main public spaces.

"There are a series of 17 sandblasted images chosen by bereaved families which have been included in this glazing so their shadows animate the interior of the building from afternoon through evening when the sun shines.

THE DUNBLANE CENTRE WINDOWS – FROM NORTH TO SOUTH

Gwen Mayor – Hedgehog
Victoria Clydesdale – Clematis
Emma Crozier – Clown drawn by Emma (also used on the No Guns record cover)
Melissa Currie – Dove holding Ballet Shoes with Laces shaped in initials 'M C'
Charlotte Dunn – Carnation
Kevin Hassell – Batman
Ross Irvine – Fox from Farthing Wood
David Kerr – Butterfly with initials 'D K' in the Wings
Mhairi McBeath – Ladybird
Brett McKinnon – Power Ranger
Abigail McLennan – Squirrel
Emily Morton – Narcissus
Sophie North – Kitkat the Cat sitting on a Kit Kat Bar
John Petrie – Tractor
Joanna Ross – Azalea
Hannah Scott – A Bunch of Daffodils
Megan Turner – Curly-haired Angel on Roller Skates with initials 'MT' on her dress

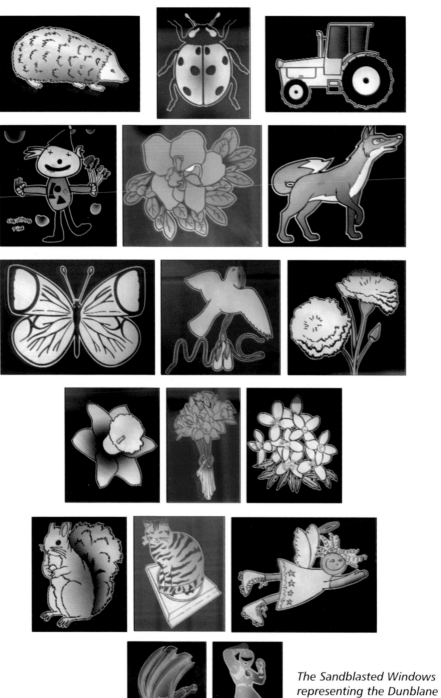

The Sandblasted Windows representing the Dunblane Victims.
(Photos: Daily Record)

(Photo: Daily Record)

"In addition, there are snowdrop images incorporated in the north-facing glazing looking towards the cathedral, the spire of which is visible from the Juice Bar. Each snowdrop image is slightly different, with gold leaf being applied to different petals or leaves, and they refer to the injured survivors of the Tragedy.

"(The Snowdrop Petition, launched by a group of concerned local mothers, developed as a successful non-political campaign – the name was chosen as the snowdrop was the only flower in bloom in Dunblane in March 1996.)

"There is a mirror inscribed by Mick North, father of Sophie, which allows for reflection as one travels down the ramp to the Sports Hall (see Chapter 10).

(Photo: Daily Record)

The Centre at Night. (Photo: Shannon Tofts)

"From the outside, particularly on dark, cold evenings, the building opens up to prospective users, with coloured lighting illuminating the dramatic ramps behind the glazing with its horizontal ('go faster stripes') emphasis and hinting at the vibrant exciting atmosphere within.

"It is our hope that the building helps young people to develop to the very best of their ability, and to have a great time as they do so!"

The project was completed on time and under budget

The building was a finalist for the RIAS (Royal Incorporation of Architects in Scotland) Andrew Doolan Best Building in Scotland Award in 2005, a prize that was won by the Scottish Parliament building.

25 SEPTEMBER 2004 – GRAND OPENING DAY

… as remembered by **Eleanor Brailsford** and **Nora Gilfillan [Dougherty]**

"After what seemed like years (actually it was years) The Centre was at long last almost ready, we were very excited and wanted to make sure the Opening was marked properly. The Community had been following the progress and updates of the project through the local free newspaper – Alan Booth who was a trustee of our project was also the editor of the Community View. We knew that there was a lot of interest in what the building looked like inside.

"A group of volunteers who had been involved with the youth clubs met and talked about what sort of format the Opening Day should take. We discussed inviting some celebrities to help make the day special. There were many suggestions, maybe a sports star or a pop star who would appeal to the young people, a media celebrity or even lots of different guests – the list seemed endless. Eventually after much discussion it was realised that there was actually no need for any famous people to come along for the Opening, this Centre had been gifted to Dunblane and the special people we wanted there were here – the inhabitants of Dunblane.

"So after years of planning The Centre, the day seemed to be hurtling towards us and many arrangements needed to be made to ensure the day was a success. Almost daily there were meetings or at least many phone calls as we tried to keep things on track and on top of the arrangements – delegation was top of our list. We decided to have the official opening at 2 o'clock and everybody was welcome. Invited guests would be asked to an earlier reception and shown round The Centre beforehand. These guests included all the bereaved families and the families of all those injured, trustees and partners, volunteers and a few other 'friends' (people who had supported and offered help to the project) and local church and school representatives. Dunblane Hydro Hotel provided a buffet and staffing for the occasion. We arranged to borrow extra tables and chairs from the various halls and churches in the town. Official invitations were printed and sent out and we were delighted by the positive response. The media interest began to rise, and press statements were organised.

"The excitement grew not only among 'The Centre family', the volunteers and the new staff, but throughout the whole community. Despite the nerves, we were quite confident that the day would run smoothly and were delighted that Mick North, who had agreed to be our founding patron would open The Centre. We had discussed letting off balloons or cutting a ribbon, and then Eleanor came up with a brilliant idea, that Mick should release doves from a basket and this would mark the official opening. It was perfect and seemed so appropriate and symbolic of everything that The Centre represented.

"Saturday 25 September arrived, and the sun shone on a superb occasion. It had been a long time since the whole community had been together to celebrate. All of the Community had been affected by the Tragedy, and it was wonderful to see so many smiling faces as hundreds of people, young and old, turned up and filled the car park. The atmosphere was happy, but you could sense people remembered why the funds had come that had made The Centre possible. After speeches from Alan Robinson, the chair of Dunblane Youth & Sports Centre Trust, and Colonel Stirling, chair of Dunblane Community Trust, Mick North, despite a little hitch when the last bird was reluctant to leave the basket, finally and successfully declared the Dunblane Centre open!

"Everybody was taken in small groups and shown round the building by one of the volunteer guides who included pupils from the High School. With all the local schools represented, either demonstrating sports or performing music the place had a buzz about it. The Centre felt alive with the sounds of laughter and excitement. Staff and volunteers were on hand to encourage people to take out memberships. Sticky badges with our new logo – which showed the initials of Dunblane Centre turned in a half circle to look like a person moving forward inside the larger circle which represents the Community – were handed out.

"For everyone who had been involved in getting The Centre open, it was a very proud and happy day and one we will never forget."

Maureen Simpson, who was appointed before Opening Day, also recalls the occasion:

"I was a volunteer in the old youth club and when there were jobs advertised for the new Centre I applied, not thinking for a minute I would get a job. But I got an interview and they asked me what I could bring to the job. I said I spoke fluent teenager so I would be ideal. They laughed and we carried on with the interview, though I think by the end I was interviewing them. It all went well and I got the job.

"On the day of the Grand Opening we the staff and volunteers were given our jobs for the day. I was going to be in the Sports Hall opening memberships. Everything was set up, we all gathered outside for the big event. It was really exciting and nerve wracking. The music from Central FM was playing, food was

Opening Ceremony; (top left) The Celebration Cake donated by the Dunblane Hydro; (top right) Signing up new Members in the Sports Hall; (bottom left) Mick North releases the Doves; (bottom right) Colonel Stirling gives his Speech with Alan Robinson and David Chisholm (trustee) to his right with Rog Jefferies (trustee) with Scott Neil (manager) behind.

being cooked. We had heard Robbie Coltrane was doing the cutting of the ribbon, that didn't happen. But with Mick North on the ball it all went to plan. We all raced inside to get to our stations and the fun began.

"No-one expected the number of people who signed up for memberships. It was amazing. I didn't think I moved for what seemed like hours. Guests were being shown round the building by young volunteers and finishing up in the Sports Hall. It was a really fabulous day, and I'm glad I was part of it."

Happily, the feedback from Opening Day was very favourable which was extremely gratifying to the many people who had worked tirelessly (an overused phrase but entirely appropriate in this case) to get us to this point.

Reflections from the Architect Ten Years On – Willie Brown Looks Back on the Dunblane Centre Project

"It is a general rule that in life it is never great to go back.

"However, this is how architects learn – sometimes painfully – that what works on a plan preserved timelessly on paper may not work in a 24-hour, three-dimensional world, such as changes of use for spaces that nobody could have predicted prior to people actually using the building itself.

"I like going back to the Dunblane Centre. I like driving by the building at 4pm on rainy November afternoons and seeing the light streaming out, energetic children running up and down the ramps facing the arrival space.

"I like seeing the beech hedge mature in the sunshine into a green protecting arm, I like seeing the Sky, BBC and STV outside-broadcast vans outside and the intense supportive atmosphere inside as Andy Murray cannons another serve down the line.

"I like that the disco space is flexible enough to hold NHS Strategy meetings – I think the DJ for that event has a tough gig!

"I even like seeing the lively hotch potch of photos and posters advertising events and performances past and future on the ramp walls, untouched by spirit level, tape measure or any graphic sensibility whatever. The shadows of the carefully positioned sandblasted images seem to glide serenely over all this, almost playfully interacting with the photos.

"It also helps with perspective when one reminds oneself of the terrible genesis of the project, and how the consultant team and contractors, inspired by the astounding bravery and dignity of the bereaved and directly affected, worked tirelessly to achieve a useful and slightly poetic building, within a very tight budget. Looking back, while the issue of cost control was an ever present concern for the client (in a construction era dominated by public outrage at the spiralling costs of the Parliament building at Holyrood) we were confident that our experienced team would deliver as they had previously on other projects together, and so it came to be.

"Our confidence was underpinned by the inspiring, exciting and constantly surprising interaction with the young people of Dunblane through the developing of the brief and we knew that we were designing a facility that was meeting a need.

"By far the most difficult area for us to deal with was not the design or procurement process, which were after all, our bread and butter, it was the creation of an appropriate memorial, subtle and sensitive, to be embedded in the building. The 17 sandblasted images were inspired by Shona McInnes's

beautiful stained glass artwork in the nearby Holy Family Church (See Chapter 2 – Local Churches)

"I hope we will be reflecting on the Dunblane Centre after 25 years, and someone else will be doing it after 50 years. It is a very rewarding endeavour to have been part of, one of the most important buildings of my career, and indeed experiences of my life, without doubt.

"There is one other person I never credited, whose contribution to the building is immense, my late wife Hilary, who lost her battle with cancer last year. Hilary would always encourage me onwards."

A framed Welcome Message, hand-painted by local Resident and Neighbour Elise MacRae.

CHAPTER 5 –
OPEN FOR BUSINESS, NO MORE TIME TO PLAN

LES MORTON
with contributions from SCOTT NEIL, PAULINE McPARLAND, TED
CHRISTOPHER, AARON FYFE, ANDY McBROOM and ANN JACKSON

AUTUMN 2004 – THE FIRST THREE MONTHS

There wasn't really time for much of a celebration because 'We Were Open' and
now seven days a week there was:
- a community to serve
- customer service standards to be established and delivered
- revenue to earn

There was no more time to plan – it was time to see if the plan would work.

We had anticipated with all the publicity surrounding the Opening that
demand would initially be high. Many people in Dunblane would be interested
in visiting the Centre and trying out the activities, even if this was only out of
curiosity. Between Opening Day on 25 September and the end of October we took
£8,682 in membership fees, well above our expectation.

However, the reality was that once the initial excitement had died down our
revenues decreased dramatically. Those for November were 63% of the October
figure, and December revenues were down a further 32%. Over a three month
period our monthly cash takings had decreased from almost £18,000 to only
£7,500. Takings for those first three months were only 72% of what we had
budgeted and, excluding the excellent result from selling memberships, the
takings from activities were even more disappointing.

A simple reporting system had been established to ensure the trustees
and manager were aware of the financial situation on a daily basis, and by
mid-November it was clear that the financial plan was not being achieved and,
worryingly, the trend was downwards. Having managed to get through to
Opening Day with very limited working capital this financial shortfall versus our
plan was not sustainable. We had a payroll to meet and bills to pay but if things
continued as they were we were going to run out of money and this was going to
happen soon. Urgent action was required.

Emergency meetings were held to examine:
- where we were falling short from the financial plan
- why we were falling short from the financial plan
- what could be done to rectify the situation

The simple truth was that after the great success of Grand Opening Day we
were suffering from a general lack of footfall i.e. paying customers. In hindsight
we had been so focused on completing the building and preparing for the
Opening that we had not spent enough time ensuring that what was on offer was

suitably attractive to our prospective customer base. Not enough information was available and, quite simply, we were not adequately organised to attract people into The Centre.

After a reasonable opening month we were falling short in all the main areas of the financial plan except one – the cost plan, where we were spending in line with expectation.

Revenue well down on plan, Costs in line with plan = Looming financial disaster

It was agreed that to boost footfall we needed better communication with the Community, to be more organised in our offering (for example, timings and charges for fitness classes and Sports Hall usage), and to develop closer relationships with the local schools. We needed to do more to make the Community aware of what was available and why they should be coming to the Dunblane Centre – and this would take time to produce significant improvements in revenues.

But if we were not to run out of cash we needed to address our cost base urgently. By far the most significant cost area was staffing. We had a staff plan which was geared to a certain level of activity and which covered customer service, supervision, equipment handling, administration and so on. But the reality was that during November and December we had staff hanging about and no customers for a large chunk of our opening hours. This was unsustainable.

There were some fraught meetings of the trustees and manager, but the inevitable outcome was that we had to restructure and reorganise staffing levels and shift patterns. In a service business the staffing must be focused primarily on customer service. Employing staff when there are no customers (or few customers) makes no financial sense, particularly when funds are limited.

Action was also taken to improve our internal authorisation procedures, particularly regarding expenditure. The trustees did not have detailed knowledge of everything that was happening day by day in The Centre and some unwise and unnecessary commitments and expenditures were made in the first couple of months. Reporting and authorisation thresholds were examined and clarified.

Every penny became a prisoner

Scott Neil recalls his time as The Centre's first manager (2004-2009):

"One of my ambitions as a youngster was to become a professional footballer or professional golfer. More realistically it was to become the manager of a sports facility. When the Dunblane Centre vacancy became available it was at the perfect time for me in my career and the fact it was a brand new facility was even better. This was a fantastic opportunity for me just past my 26th birthday.

Scott Neil on a Staff Team Building Day.

"I will always remember my first day of work. It was four months prior to The Centre opening. The first task was to start up the PC in the office. It took at least 30 minutes to load up – some start! Next job was to take a first look at the activity programme, pricing, staffing levels, procedures etc. We were starting from nothing with 'a blank piece of paper'. That was the beginning of the most exciting journey for me. Over the first year, but particularly during those first few months, there were many occasions when I thought "why did I take this job?". There was challenge after challenge with most becoming harder not easier by the day. But on reflection I can now look back and laugh, and the experience made me a stronger person.

"That first year was scary. The project had to be successful, The Centre well used and financially viable. There were income targets to be met which meant maximising adult bookings that generated much needed higher income whilst trying to keep costs to young people to a minimum, one of The Centre's guiding principles. It was challenging to get the right balance, but from my point of view it had to work financially to ensure all costs were met and this was not always popular.

"With an empty timetable to start with activities were added in wherever there were volunteers to run them, but I also tried to meet any demand from the local community for activities which did not require resources and would be an income generator. I planned for users of all ages.

"In pre-school there was soft play, arts and music makers, which were all successes. For the young people there were youth clubs from Primary 5 to Secondary 4. These were very popular, especially with the Primary 6 and 7 age group. There was youth drop-in for the over-8s. Various groups hired the facilities for coaching sessions for children – basketball, athletics, football, karate and dance school were all extremely well attended.

"For adults there was an excellent fitness class programme, which was a massive success and an excellent income generator for The Centre, and activities were set up for retired members of the Community with a range of different session topics. Shortly after the Opening an events group was set up to organise various events through the year (see Chapter 6).

"I was impressed by the number of volunteers who put so much time, energy and effort into The Centre over the years. At one point there were 70 active volunteers from different backgrounds, jobs, abilities and ages. They were involved with youth clubs, fundraising events, pre-school activities, administration, trustees, reception, gardening, the kitchen and food preparation, marketing, sports and much more.

"Among the major successes for me were the junior volunteers. Several months after the Opening I remember suggesting at a trustees' meeting that we introduce young people to assist with youth clubs, events, kitchen help etc. Once a few of the trustees had got over the shock of the idea, junior volunteers became an integral part of The Centre. One of our stipulations was that they had to be at Secondary School and over 12 years of age. There was no stopping two of our regular young users. No sooner had the bell rung at the end of their Primary School days than they had handed in their junior volunteer application forms. It was fantastic and really gave the impression of a community project.

"One of my riskier ideas was to raise funds for The Centre by running in the 2006 Edinburgh marathon. Completing the 26.2 miles had seemed a good idea at the time and I just survived. But the fact that I managed to raise over £2,000 made it feel better.

"Looking back on my five years as The Centre's first manager I feel privileged to have had the opportunity to be there as it transformed from a building site to an exciting facility developing a busy and successful activity programme as it became part of the Community. I had enormously high levels of job satisfac-

Scott Neil's Leaving Party.

tion, and seeing The Centre break even financially and run successfully meant everything and was worth all the hours of work. I was very proud not only of my own work but also of all the volunteers, staff, instructors and Centre supporters.

"Being asked to contribute to a book to mark the Tenth Anniversary was strange as sometimes it feels as if it was just a few weeks ago that The Centre opened its doors for the first time.

"There were lots of highlights for me over the years but here are the most important:
• The Centre becoming financially viable so quickly and maintaining positive financial trading

- *The range of users of all ages*
- *The range and success of fundraising events*
- *The positive reputation the Centre gained in the local community"*

Pauline McParland was another person appointed before The Centre opened:

"My interview at the Dunblane Centre was back in August 2004. I had been approached and asked if I would like to come and work at the new Youth Centre opening in Dunblane. When I arrived for the interview, internal building work was still on-going, and so with a hard hat on and stepping over builders' equipment, I made my way to the Art Room for the interview. I was offered the post of cleaning assistant working 16 hours a week. At first, custom was slow and my job was trying to keep The Centre clean (this was mainly from the builders' dust and dirt). Other duties included taking care of all cleaning equipment and the purchase of cleaning products to comply with safety requirements. It was a mop and bucket at first, and extremely hard work, but we later purchased a buffing machine which required a degree of expertise and a sense of humour before it was mastered!

"In a year or so business was picking up, new staff joined and I progressed to working on the front desk as well as cleaning. There were fitness classes, dance classes and football, then two art classes, for children and adults. I decided to join the Thursday adult art class which was an enjoyable experience where I picked up all different types of art skills – I even had some of my paintings framed!

"I later started up a class of my own teaching jewellery-making and also helped teach some of the girls at the Youth Club and during the Holiday Programme.

"Nora Dougherty [Gilfillan] and her friend Jill Hall started offering business lunches which I helped with. Through doing this I acquired a certificate for Food Hygiene along the way and later on Lynn Balman and I took over this role.

"Another Centre assistant I worked with found out her little girl had leukaemia, so The Centre decided to do some fundraising to help them go home to Hungary for her treatment. I'm glad to say the treatment was a success, and they came back to visit and thank us for our help and support. Whenever possible, The Centre was keen to support other causes too and among others helped Changing Faces, a charity which is dear to me and my husband.

"When I joined The Centre I had only been in Scotland 18 months and knew very few people, but by the time I retired in 2011, having spent seven really great years working in a friendly and rewarding environment, I had made many new and special friendships".

Without the dedication of a huge number of people we would simply never have succeeded in creating the Dunblane Centre. To me Pauline epitomised what The Centre was all about – she was completely dedicated, happy to turn her hand to any task that had to be done, rarely complained and always had a smile on her face. Far from 'merely' being responsible for keeping the place clean and tidy, she was 'Wonder Woman' as she took bookings by phone and in person, organised deliveries, communicated with the trustees about problems that required decisions, gave directions to passing visitors who were lost - the list is endless. At the party to mark her retirement I was delighted to witness the love felt by everybody for Pauline.

(l) Pauline McParland and Les Morton;
(r) The Centre thanks Pauline on her
Retirement – 2011.

2005 – THE CENTRE ENTERS CALMER WATERS

As we moved into January 2005 much had still to be proved regarding our ability to run The Centre successfully. An operating loss of almost £11,000 had been reported for the first quarter which ended on 31 December 2004. However, as the weeks passed we were able to create a better flow of customers and to maintain customer service standards on the reduced staffing levels. Revenues increased every month from January to March as we became more organised and, indeed, more confident with what was happening.

An Events Committee was established to make sure that we were offering the proper and desirable activities and to make suggestions regarding additions to the programme. This was a very successful move and targeted the core issue that would determine success or failure – how to get paying customers through the door.

The remaining three quarters of 2005 each produced an operating profit so that overall the first year of operation had produced a small surplus of £1,673. Anyone who predicted in January 2005 that this would be the outcome for the first year would have been looked at in a very strange way.

In addition to the various activities that generated our core revenues we also had income from donations and fundraising which helped keep us solvent. There were generous gifts of money from local people and organisations such as the Dunblane New Golf Club.

An early supporter, local musician **Ted Christopher**, describes more about the No Guns Record Fund (see Chapter 2) and how it came to provide equipment for the new Centre:

"The week before Christmas 1996 we sat in John and Alison Crozier's house listening to the Top Twenty Countdown programme on Radio One. There was a huge cheer when it was announced "and straight in at number 1 is the children of Dunblane singing 'Knockin' On Heaven's Door'/'Throw These Guns Away'". The room was full of ecstatic kids and proud adults.

"When I conceived the idea of a song for Dunblane, it was never intended as a charity record or even a tribute to those killed and injured. It was simply a protest song, a song to say "Enough! This must never happen again."

CD Sleeve with Photos of the Singers and Musicians from Dunblane.

Against the advice of the record company I insisted the singers and musicians should be from Dunblane. They found it difficult to grasp that the message had to come from the town itself. The public got it. They took the record to their hearts and the media immediately recognised that. It quickly became obvious that its sales were going to raise a huge amount of money and so we set up a registered charity No Guns Record Ltd to administer these funds.

"I like to think our efforts helped in the public clamour to tighten the UK's gun laws, and on that level alone I was satisfied it had done its job. We didn't set out to raise money but nevertheless it meant that kids' charities in Britain benefited by more than half a million pounds. However, the most important and up-lifting result of the recording was one none of us had foreseen or planned. For the first time in months Dunblane was smiling.

"As trustees of the charity we saw this and felt we should contribute some of the residual funds to Dunblane's future. Music raised the money so we felt

Ted Christopher with a Group of Dunblane Children including some who sang on the Record.

there was no better way to contribute than to create an opportunity to make music in Dunblane. And thus we came to fund equipping the rehearsal and recording facilities in the new Dunblane Centre.

"On a personal note, it was a privilege to be present the day The Centre was opened. My own kids have spent many happy hours there. It really has become an integral part of the Community these ten years and I'm sure it will continue to be for many to come. It's great to pass by and see the car park full and realise the place is full of people having fun.

Children enjoying the Music Room as are (below, l-r) Duncan Johnston, Bernd Marquardt and John McClymont.

"Although I never set out to write a tribute song I believe what it helped to achieve was a fitting tribute to the whole community. I've watched as the kids who sang on it have grown into fine young adults and I'm proud to still call them friends. Now it's their generation's kids that are starting to use The Centre and they can truly say "That's ours!"

"Throw these guns away, let the children play in a safer day" say the bairns of Dunblane"

Singer songwriter **Aaron Fyfe** was one of those able to take advantage of The Centre's music facilities:

"As teenagers my friends Andrew Kerr, David Tait, James Seaman and I started a band called Fused. We played in James' parents' garage and 'entertained' the neighbours through the summer as we practised for Battle of the Bands competitions. The Dunblane Centre offered the resource of a soundproof studio, much to the delight of the boys and probably the local residents! The band's excitement at the prospect of moving from the drummer's garage to a properly equipped studio was immense. Fused was the first group to use the studio and was one of the first bands to use The Centre for a local gig. My teenage years in the Music Studio have

helped me on my musical journey. I am now a singer songwriter and have just released a new EP. I am extremely grateful to all of those involved in providing the funds and support for the Dunblane Centre and hope it will continue to inspire other young people in the future."

Andy McBroom has been a User, a Volunteer, Centre Assistant and is now a Youth Worker and was among the first group of teenagers to experience what The Centre could offer:

"My journey with the Dunblane Centre started before the facility even opened...

"As a Primary School pupil in Dunblane in the early 2000s, I went to Youth Club every week during the school term. Youth Club, held in the Duckburn Estate at the time (see Chapters 3 and 4), was what you did every week. It was almost as mandatory as eating your dinner. It was another fantastic chance to get away from home and the moans of Mum and Dad. Everyone was there for the same reason - to have a laugh. It was somewhere away from school that wasn't anything like the Scouts, Guides, Boys' Brigade or Cadets. It was like the playground, but you could be more yourself. You got to tell each other the secrets that had been murmured around the playground all day but never said out loud in case a teacher heard you. It was a place you could feel comfortable and have the best banter.

"I remember, vividly, the first time I met Scott Neil. He was brought in to meet all of the young people, and he asked us what colours we would like the walls to be. Immediately, we all said we wanted them to be pink! He also questioned us on what we liked most about the current Youth Club, looking to adopt its best parts for the new facility. As time went by we began to see the building on Stirling Road take shape, and I remember coming back to school after the 2004 summer holidays and the buzz starting to go around as we counted the days until The Centre opened.

"At the Opening on 25 September my family and I signed up as members. Looking around for the first time, I could tell that I would be spending a lot of time there. Little did I know that ten years later I would still be involved. As Youth Clubs at The Centre started up, I remember the excitement my friends and I were experiencing. We had a whole new area to play with, and best of all there was more space to use with always a room to accommodate what we wanted to do – whether it be football, a disco or paint some terrible pictures.

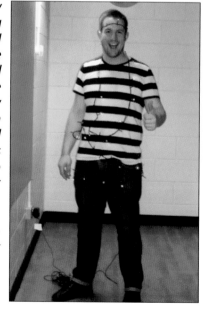

"When I was 14, I put in my application to volunteer at The Centre. I'd always felt strongly about giving back and the Youth Clubs and The Centre itself had given me so much. I started off volunteering twice a

week – one day in the Youth Club and the other as a general assistant. Youth volunteers had the privilege of wearing a 'lovely' yellow T-shirt so that the customers would recognise we were a part of the team. Safe to say, I was not disappointed when we no longer had to wear them.

"**Volunteer Day Out – 2007**. This was the day Bob Dale filled a car load with junior volunteers (whether that's how many junior volunteers we had, or we were just the committed ones, I don't know), and took us to Xscape in Braehead for the day as a 'thank you' for our hard work. It was a fun-filled day with rock climbing, high-ropes course and enough pizza to 'feed the 5000' Not long after that, we received letters home thanking us for our valued service. It's small things like that which make you feel appreciated and keep you coming back for more.

"**Youth Committee** – Early on Bob had a fantastic idea to put together a Youth Committee for The Centre. The plan was to gather a maximum of ten young people who were regular users and to meet monthly to discuss plans about what the local young people could benefit from at The Centre including what events we should run and what new equipment we should buy. The committee met until 2008.

"During my time volunteering Scott Neil always said that I should apply for a job at The Centre when I turned 16. Although I knew he could never give me any guarantee, the thought of working at The Centre stuck in my head and I committed myself to keep volunteering until I would be old enough to apply. Then two years later, around the time of my 16th birthday, The Centre wanted to hire two relief assistants. Just a coincidence? .... Probably.

"It was an extremely happy day for me when I found out that I had been employed by The Centre. It was my first paid job and in a place that I loved, with people that I enjoyed being around. From what I know now, being a member of staff at the Dunblane Centre is very, very different from working in other places. It's more of a family atmosphere and you get to have fun at the same time as you're working. It was first and foremost a centre for the community and I was able to build relationships with the customers. And unlike some places, where a customer is just a customer, I am still able to engage with the same ladies who came to fitness classes more than six years ago. It's a facility with a fantastic memory.

"Working in The Centre for the next four years really shaped who I was as a person. Being involved so closely in so many aspects of The Centre's life really helped me gain confidence in customer care and dealing with the public, skills without which I would not have been

Andy McBroom 'working' at Reception.

able to get the various jobs I've had though still holding my relief position at The Centre.

"In 2013 I was lucky enough to be employed as the Youth Worker while Jeannie Gray took her maternity leave. It was an odd feeling coming back to The Centre on a full-time basis, and also viewing the place from a different angle. I have loved being back here, it almost feels like being 16 again. In this new position I have realised that the young people I once worked with are now a lot older and have gone. There are, however, always new, younger children moving in and using The Centre's facilities. There will always be a key relationship between The Centre and the young people of Dunblane, a relationship I saw begin when The Centre opened and one I love seeing continue to grow! I am very much looking forward to seeing how it will develop over the next ten years."

DECEMBER 2005 – DUNBLANE CENTRE TO THE RESCUE

Ann Jackson, a volunteer on the Events Group, describes how her involvement with The Centre began:

"In 2005 I was the manager of Arnhall Nursery in Dunblane and a few days before Christmas the main building was destroyed by fire. Fortunately no one was in the nursery at the time. Our main priority was to find a venue in order to continue our nursery service. This was when the Dunblane Centre came to our rescue and offered us the use of the facilities. This was the perfect solution to our situation and was convenient for all our families. Two days after the fire The Centre became our temporary nursery for the older children whilst the younger ones remained at an unaffected building at the nursery. The Centre's office became my base for the duration of our stay and I enjoyed being part of the buzz of The Centre's goings-on.

"Many of the children based at The Centre are now teenagers and probably do not remember the happy time they spent there. They enjoyed having the opportunity to visit the shops, park and library as everything was easy to walk to. Scott never had a shortage of willing assistants to help him put out the soft play equipment in the Sports Hall. Lots of fun was had there!

"I met so many lovely people using The Centre and the staff, management and trustees were so accommodating and friendly towards the invasion of our $2^1/_2$ - 4-year-old children and our staff. Although we were looking forward to returning to our temporary Portakabins, we were all rather sad to leave The Centre as it had been such a happy and fun time for everyone and we could not have asked for a better venue to continue operating the nursery during a challenging time.

"I had seen how much The Centre offered to all ages of our community and *wanted to contribute in some way. And so as a result of a most unusual turn of events I became a volunteer. Being part of the Events Group has been rewarding and we have arranged many events to raise money for the continuation of such a special place in our community. Happy 10th Birthday!"*

AN ANECDOTE FROM LES

Scott organised a 5-a-side football competition for under-16s teams. An additional team was required to even up the draw so it was decided that a team would be entered representing Centre staff and volunteers (none of whom was under 16). We modestly named ourselves 'The Centre All Stars' and reached the final of the competition where we were to play a team of youngsters whose speed and energy levels were to us 'breathtaking'. Bill Stewart, captain of 'The Centre All Stars' was 60, I was 53, Bob Dale, Scott Neil and Andy McBroom were young but could hardly be described as 'footballers' and our ambition in the final was to finish it alive and breathing. At half-time there was a 5-minute break and I went to reception to get some water. Standing a few yards away chatting animatedly was the 'opposition', unhappy to be losing 3-1 and whose summary of their predicament was "c'mon guys, these people are absolutely ancient, let's run the legs off them in the second half, they'll be needing oxygen soon" (expletives deleted!).

Final result – 7-5 to the 'Centre All Stars' – Ye cannae beat an Auld Heid!

2006 – CONCLUDING ON A POSITIVE NOTE

We submitted quarterly financial reports to the trustees of the Dunblane Community Trust (DCT) who obviously had a keen interest in how we were faring. The report to the end of December 2004 had not made good reading, but we out-lined the decisions that had been made to address the problems and expressed confidence that things would improve soon. For the remainder of that first year DCT donated a total of £30,000 in revenue support, a figure that was repeated the following year and which was gratefully accepted. Although we could not rely on this continuing revenue support from DCT, the transfer of money to our bank account meant that we did not have to worry constantly about paying the bills. We had made tough decisions that would ensure we could operate The Centre successfully but this substantial donation of £60,000 over the first two years gave us a financial cushion which enabled us to move The Centre forward with much more confidence.

- We learned quickly what worked and what did not work
- We added events and activities
- We developed youth programmes
- We ensured that the staff and volunteers felt involved in every major decision

- We strived to provide Dunblane with a facility of which local people could be proud and befitting its origins

Nobody ever forgot the repeated message from Bob Jack, on behalf of Stirling Council, that whatever the outcome, whatever was built, whatever problems ensued – these were the responsibility of The Centre's trustees alone.

A fantastic community facility was the outcome

A unique building was created

Dozens of significant problems ensued and were overcome

And ten years later –
well done the People of Dunblane – we're still going strong

A FEW REMINDERS FROM THOSE EARLY DAYS

..... including Red Nose Day organised at a week's notice!

The Centre celebrates its Second Anniversary – the first Funday Sunday, September 2006 – (l-r) Nancy McLaren, Scott Neil, Nora Dougherty [Gilfillan], Louise Dawson, John McLaren, Katy Oliver, Margaret Sharkey, Bob Dale, Eric Simpson, Steve Birnie, Kenny Fraser and Maureen Simpson.

CHAPTER 6 – THE LIFE AND SOUL OF THE CENTRE

BOB DALE, PAMELA MACKIE, PAM ROSS and NORA GILFILLAN
with contributions from KENNY FRASER, ANN MURDOCH and ROSIE MASON

The Life and Soul of The Dunblane Centre is and always will be its people, those who organise, those who participate, everyone gaining through its activities and events. Here, in the words of some key people in The Centre's life, and with a selection of photos from the past ten years, is a flavour of what Dunblane has been able to enjoy through its special gift.

BOB DALE – FORMER DC YOUTH WORKER WHO IS STILL INVOLVED IN MANY OF THE CENTRE'S ACTIVITIES:

Where to start ....
- 3 Youth Clubs a week
- 10 Summer Programmes
- 20 Musical Performances
- 3 Sleepovers
- 1 Beach Party (never again!)
- Christmas Balls
- Halloween Parties

.... the list goes on. Being me, I procrastinated and decided to begin by looking through over 4,000 photos I've taken of all the activities over the years. That seemed easier than sitting down and planning to write anything! I'm going through all the shows, the programmes and drop-ins that happened during my time at The Centre.

To start with I suppose I should say who I am.... I'm Bob and I had the genuine pleasure of being the youth worker at The Centre for six years, that's long enough to see some of the very young children become staff! At the beginning I was quite young myself, but having been brought up in Dunblane I knew how important and influential The Centre was in the lives of children and young people then and would be forever.

When most young people think of activities at The Centre they remember the big events like the sleepovers and the summer shows, but there are hundreds of other activities that go on, and I'd like to share my memories of how some of them began and grew and are still going.

When I started at The Centre I had, with the help of the manager, to redesign the youth programme from scratch, and this allowed us to plan events and activities that had either not been tried or even been thought of before. In some cases I wish I'd never thought of them either! A number of these were what would be called 'normal activities' – Youth Club football and table tennis tournaments and Dunblane Centre's Got Talent. However, I always tried to look for something a bit different that the staff team could get behind, and I must say I always had great support from the staff (or 'dream team' as they like to be known) when it came to the big events – they all wanted a go.

Some of my favourite events happened because other people were willing to give up their time to come in to speak to and interact with the young people and

not because they were doing the work! We had biodiversity week in which under instruction the young people were digging around in the garden looking for bugs and wildlife – it's amazing what was found in what was essentially the waste pile from the building's foundations. In conjunction with Stirling Council we had a visit from an ex-offender who talked with our older group about knife crime, a really powerful night that I hope lives on in the

Biodiversity Week.

young people's minds as long as it will in mine.

One of the biggest events on The Centre's calendar happens in September each year, Funday Sunday – that's The Centre's birthday! It's always a great day and sees The Centre as we always want it to be, full of people, fun and atmosphere. Personally I will hope to be going to Funday Sunday for decades to come!

All the Fun of Funday Sunday.

Now to share memories of some specific events that went on in the Youth Programme. And where better to start than with the one event that, no matter what, I will never repeat – the Beach Party! Well what do you say, it was one of these crazy ideas that formed in my head. I thought it would be great to throw a summer-themed party/event for the 12-16 year olds and use the whole Centre. It was not the first time we had taken over the whole building (see below). Up until this point all the activities had been what I would class as a great success - that requires both the young people and the staff/volunteers enjoying themselves and all thinking it was a success. By that measure the

The Beach Party.

Beach Party was half a success as the young people (and Andy McBroom) did have a great night. The simple logistics were to get two tonnes of sand and dump that in the Function Room, get the largest paddling/smallest swimming pool and pop that out the back of the building and then run some 'beachy' type games and activities, with some bingo, and you've got yourself a wonderful night that every-one can take happy memories away from. Alas we didn't think about how long it would take to get two tonnes of sand in or out of the Function Room, we didn't plan on running out of water because we'd filled the pool and drained the tank dry (notice I have now started using 'we' and not 'I') and then having to sit and have a chat with all the staff about which trustee to phone! Sand and water mix really well and spread, oh my how the mix spreads. So by the end of the night we had sand and water everywhere, no water for cleaning up (not even just an excuse this time!) and lots of very cold and wet young people who had had a blast. It's possible to look back and forget the hours of wheeling barrows full of sand in and out, dealing with water shortages and the pile of sand that was in the back garden for months and simply remember that there were 60 young people who left that night with memories for life! Matt Birnie also shares his memories of this in Chapter 7.

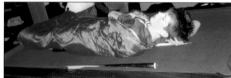

The first time we had used the whole of The Centre for an event was for what we called our Lock-In. And it was the biggest event that I had ever organised as a youth worker. To this day I am still asked about it by young people, those who were present and even those who didn't get a chance to go. Lock-In started off as a wild idea that I never really thought would go anywhere but to my surprise a few weeks later I'm there planning a programme for the evening.... what games to play, what DVDs to get in, how much food to bring and who is daft enough to come and work all night with 50 young people! The staff were always keen when-ever they thought they would enjoy an activity, and so we had staff members 'ready to go'. All we needed to do was get the young people involved. I never thought

The Lock-Ins.

we would get such a positive response from parents and young people and we were sold out in no time. We had the activities planned, the movies rented and volunteers coming in to gee us all up throughout. It was a great night and an absolute pleasure to attend; not only was it great fun but it allowed the young people, staff and volunteers to build a great rapport that remains to this day. The best outcome was that Lock-Ins have become a regular part of the programme and are still going on.

Perhaps the biggest success that we have would be the shows, Show in a Week and the Pantos, which have been shining successes for both the youth programme and the cultural life of The Centre. And there is no other time that I will get to dress up as a fairy and prance around!

PAMELA MACKIE TELLS THE STORY OF THE SHOWS

I vaguely remember sitting down in spring 2006 with Scott Neil (who was then manager of The Centre) and proposing that we try putting on a summer musical for kids, from P1 upwards, in one week during the summer holidays. Scott didn't like theatre much (and in fact at that point had never seen a musical – if he had he might not have been so receptive to the blatantly ridiculous idea) but thought it would be a good way of  getting some young people in The Centre over the often quiet summer period. In fact we had a bet on that we wouldn't get 50 signed up (my then maximum numbers!). We did and thus with the little known (but fabulous) show 'Seussical' and a fair amount of making things up as we went along from myself and Bob Dale, **Show in a Week** was born. All these years on and both Show in a Week and indeed performing arts at The Centre have grown beyond anything I ever thought it might be, from the initial 50 kids on the primary school staging with a few borrowed lights in 2006 to 'King and I' seven years later – 118 kids, a massive

Three of Pamela's 'Budding Thespians'.

stage, lighting and sound kit and two beautifully painted elephants. Along the way we've added a still growing annual Panto, some shows for adults with our grown up cast (including one outdoors), a few concerts and of course our show choir. For all the growth in scale though, the premise remains the same. Theatre and performance is an amazing experience – and I would like to make that available to as many young people as I possibly can, in as positive a way as we can make it.

On a personal level the shows and the young people have had a huge impact on my life. When we started

I just had Holly who was then five. Now I have three more little budding thespians – each of whom has been born into a huge extended family of kids and young people always willing to play/cuddle/entertain as appropriate. The shows and their casts are a massive part of all our lives and one that I wouldn't be without. The young people who take part in the shows never cease to amaze me – what they pull off in a short space of time is incredible and the sense of teamwork and looking out for each other is always wonderful to see. To see them grow over such a long period of time is a true privilege.

It would be remiss not to mention my wonderful troop of adults who come to perform, teach, lead, support and encourage our young company. By my count we've had over 40 adult performers involved over the years with people travelling from as far afield as London and even Denmark to take part. They all give their time to help with the shows and we absolutely couldn't do it without them.

When I wrote the programme for the Show of Shows (see Chapter 8) I asked both the kids and the adults if they had any memories or stories they wanted included and I only realised when I came to write this how difficult it is to pick one or two memories out of such a huge range of experiences. From half the cast wandering about The Centre sporting various plaster casts (Seussical) to cuddling an actual real life zebra (Just So), from chasing our awol 'Toto' over half of Dunblane (Wizard of Oz) to painting Leigh green (Aladdin) and from making over 100 enchanted object costumes, a wardrobe, clock and dear knows what else while very, very heavily pregnant (Beauty and the Beast) to doing tea runs in the middle of the night to the poor tech boys who slept in a van to keep an eye on the outside equipment (Into the Woods), watching/empathising with the guys going above and beyond and getting waxed/tanned (The King and I) to the hugely emotional 'rubber chickens' at the end of the show when the kids are all both hyper and exhausted (pretty much every show). The shows at The Centre have given me and hopefully everyone who has been involved in them in any capacity – on the stage, in the band, backstage, working at The Centre, in the audience – a wealth of memories.

The Crew of the USS Albatross –Stardate 6.08.2012 (Return to the Forbidden Planet).
(Photo: Louise Bellen)

Return to the Forbidden Planet (2012).

Jack and the Beanstalk (2010).

Babes in the Wood (2011).

Fame (2013).

Beauty and the Beast (2011).

Little Shop of Horrors (2010).

Into the Woods (2013).

Jack and the Beanstalk (2010); Dick Whittington (2012); Cinderella (2009).

King and I (2013).

Just So (2008).

A Selection of Images Illustrating the Vibrancy, Vivacity and Variety of The Centre's Productions.

The Centre is 10 this year, hence marking the huge amount we have achieved in the performing arts in that time – we didn't stop with the Show of Shows, there is 'Oliver' in the summer, an adult production of 'Elegies for Angels, Punks and Raging Queens' in November plus Panto at Christmas, then our Tenth Show in a Week in 2015. The future is looking hugely exciting and I hope very much that everyone will be a part of it.

BOB DALE AGAIN

Everything we have ever put on as an activity has always been to ensure that the children and young people benefit, but it has always been the ethos at The Centre to help to integrate the young people in to the community of Dunblane. This is no more evident than in the great work of DYPP (Dunblane Young People's Project). This group came together to manage a fund of money to benefit the town's young people. They are the best group I have ever worked with, their drive and commitment is testament to how well young people can work together and prove what they're capable of, not only to the adults around them but also to themselves. They managed to run a survey to find out what the local people wanted and gained over 100 responses, and I am delighted to say that they managed to hand out £65,000 to support great projects in the local area. DYPP funds provided the original soft play equipment for The Centre and more recently secured the future of the Saturday Night Project with a donation of £25,000 (see Chapter 9).

I have been involved in and had the chance to run many things through The Centre, from watching young people host a fantastic Burns Supper every year to taking 85 lively 9- and 10-year-olds to the cinema (what a great way to get out of a double booking!) and spending 24 hours in the place without going any more stark raving mad than I was to begin with! Don't get me wrong it's not all been great days and rainbows, but the days that shine through, and the ones that the young people will remember, have been the best and will live with me for ages.

The more I look through those photos the more I remember and I can say with my hand on my heart that the role of youth worker within The Centre has been my favourite job and is always likely to remain so. I have the pleasure of going back and helping out with different events from time to time, nowadays without having any hair-brained ideas about what events to put on, and to see the young people (most of whom are adults now!).

I will conclude by saying that ten years on The Centre is still a vibrant and exciting place to be for people of all ages and can be everything from a place to hang out after school to somewhere that can bridge age and generation gaps. Places with such a diverse remit and client base are few and far between and to have one in Dunblane that is as fun to be in now as it was the day it opened is a huge asset to the town and its people. I will be going back to volunteer for things again and again and here's hoping there are many more stupid ideas for events because they are the ones that build memories, and that's the best legacy The Centre can have.

I would like to express my huge gratitude to all the volunteers who help at all the events that go on at the Dunblane Centre, in whatever capacity, those who helped provide bacon rolls for 50 young people, those who shovelled sand and especially those who gave up their time week in and week out. Without them none of the activities would have been possible... so thanks from the bottom of my heart.

PAM ROSS AND NORA GILFILLAN DESCRIBE THE VALUE OF VOLUNTEERS AND SUPPORTERS

This book wouldn't be complete without us paying tribute to every single Dunblane Centre volunteer and supporter – past, present or future. The original vision of a youth facility began with a group of volunteers. Their ideas and dedication to see the project through were the reasons we have the Dunblane Centre, and now today's volunteers who support the Centre manager and staff are the reason it continues to thrive.

The gift of The Centre didn't come from any one company or a rich benefactor, but from people who just wanted to help the Dunblane community ease their pain. It is fitting that by volunteering, local people are themselves gifting their time and this is perhaps the best way of showing their thanks and appreciation for the gift of The Centre.

Everyone with time to spare, whether it's half an hour or half a day, a regular slot or a one-off, is welcomed into a very informal and relaxed atmosphere. In The Centre we rely in no small way on a very generous army of volunteers and supporters, young and old (12-80+ yrs!!). They turn their hands to all sorts of things. Some are happy to help behind the scenes, in the kitchen or tuck shop and others like being a face to help and say hello at reception. The regular fundraising events are planned and run by the team in the Events Group. The weekly Youth Clubs and Saturday Night Project depend on both junior and adult helpers for supervision, our pre-school art and craft and music classes are organised and run by volunteers and the trustees are also all volunteers. We have people who help with gardening, DIY and maintenance, making costumes, props and scenery for shows or in the office doing admin jobs. They offer inspired ideas, they encourage others to get involved, they bring their families and friends along to all sorts of fun and exciting occasions and willingly show their loyal support by sponsoring events or donating prizes, soup, plants or homebaking!

Not only does The Centre reap the benefit of such valuable help, skills and generosity, but for the volunteers there are benefits too. Volunteering provides an opportunity to meet and make new friends. Relationships are nurtured as adult volunteers have the chance to get to know, recognise and interact with our local young people, rather than to feel threatened by groups who are doing nothing worse than 'hanging out' together.

Long term volunteer **Kenny Fraser** agrees:

> *"I have met a lot of good people, which I otherwise wouldn't have done, and had a great time at quiz nights and the like. But most of all, I have enjoyed seeing the kids from the Youth Club growing up into young adults, meeting them in the street and having them smile and say "hello".*
>
> *"I would like to think we have given them their own place to hang out, be safe, and just have fun together."*

All age groups are able to discover fresh talents and learn or improve communication skills. It can offer a sense of belonging and a sense of purpose within the Community. And what better way to see different generations grow comfortable and at ease with one another.

One of those to bridge the generation gap is **Ann Murdoch**.

> *"I began as a volunteer at The Centre in 2006. I had become involved through bringing my grandchildren to attend various activities. As I was new to Dunblane I decided to look for volunteering work here. Being a volunteer has been one of my most fulfilling experiences. I have always been welcomed and thanked by the staff for my services. I really enjoy the work on reception and interacting with people who use The Centre. My favourite part is seeing the*

children enjoying themselves at Soft Play and attending Youth Club. Being here has made me feel part of the Community, and I am so grateful to be involved in this worthwhile charity which offers so much to Dunblane."

The volunteers see the results of their constant help and hard work in the day-to-day running of activities and regular events, and when they see the smiles on everyone's faces, particularly the children, they know it has been worthwhile. They have every right to be extremely proud of their efforts and commitment, as we are of them, and in recognition of this Dunblane Centre volunteers were awarded Best Group of Volunteers by Stirling Volunteer Centre in 2006. When this award was received Susan Kerr said this was her proudest moment as a volunteer.

Friday June 9th 2006

DUNBLANE CENTRE

Dear Susan

It's official - you're the best!

Although we always knew we had the best volunteers we could hope for, it was great to have this recognised by others this week.

Following a county-wide look at community organisations, Stirling Volunteers Centre (SVC) has declared the Dunblane Centre volunteers as 'Best Group of Volunteers'.

This annual award is judged by the Chief Executive of Volunteer Development Scotland, the Editor of the Stirling Observer, the Chair of SVC's Board of Directors and the former Head of Stirling Council's Community Services. Criteria applied included the impact the work has on the community, the commitment of volunteers and the achievement of the work. We found out we'd won earlier this week and attached to this letter is a copy of the award certificate, with a trophy at the Centre.

Congratulations and thank you for your personal efforts in making this happen. It's a great achievement and only possible thanks to the tireless work put in by you and all our volunteers. You are the heart of this Centre and this is your award. I hope you're as proud of it as we are of you.

We plan to have a volunteers' event later this year to celebrate our achievements to date and. we hope you will be able to come along and join us. By then we'll also know if we've been successful in Stirling Council's 'Provost Civic Awards'

In the meantime, our thanks again for everything you do for the Centre, and for Dunblane's community. Please keep on encouraging others to get involved, especially with youth clubs and the Saturday night project.

With best wishes,

Scott

Scott Neil
On behalf of the Centre Management

We are delighted to be able to offer a channel to young people who are undertaking their Duke of Edinburgh Awards, giving them various tasks in order to achieve the required hours for the volunteering section of their award. We are proud to support people who have learning or physical disabilities, others who find themselves needing a stepping stone into or back to work or who are getting back into circulation after illness. And we have those who are retired or whose children are at school and are looking to do something useful to fill their time. It is so encouraging and rewarding to see The Centre's 'family' help others to come out of themselves, increase their confidence and abilities or use their experience to further their own lives or careers.

Our volunteers complement a manager, staff and instructor team of 24 (mainly part–time), and currently we have around 50 adult and 30 junior volunteers (12 recently as part of their Duke of Edinburgh Award). It might be surprising to know that if staff were paid to do the equivalent hours our volunteers give, it would increase our wage bill by at least £40,000 per year!

There will always be a need for people to take up this special role and there is no doubt that without our volunteers The Centre would not have the 'life and soul' that it transmits, and they would lose out on the sense of ownership and responsibility that is felt about such an exceptional place.

Volunteer Fergus Gordon with Jeannie Gray (Centre Youth Worker, l), Lynda Young and Elaine Fotheringham (both with Stirling Council Youth Services).

... AND THE ROLE OF THE STAFF

The jobs of Centre Manager and Centre Assistant are simply not like any other 'ordinary jobs'. Even the job titles themselves don't describe or truly reflect the sheer scope of what these jobs at times entail! Because of the unique nature of The Centre, it could be said that the staff are, in effect, acting as custodians of the gift which has been entrusted to them, with the promise that they make available and share with everyone, the activities and services that both meet the needs of the local people as well as ensuring that The Centre continues to be able to operate.

This sounds like a heavy responsibility and something which no-one can afford to be complacent about, having an obligation not to waste resources and hard earned operating funds.

There are no doubt times when they must wonder why they took the job or got involved at all! But the best part is that it is such a happy, relaxed and informal environment to work in, and that the challenges are faced with a conscientious and positive approach, a team spirit and a sense of humour! There is a great 'family' atmosphere about the place, which is just as well since, as often as not, partners, children and parents all get sucked or roped in to being involved in some way or other!

Every shift and every day is different. There can be business meetings to cater for or badminton nets to put up; it could be a day of setting everything up for a Craft Fair or doing the clear-up after a busy Youth Club. It might be making coffee or putting away a giant bouncy castle. One minute you could be climbing ladders putting up an advertising banner for the forthcoming Panto, cleaning toilets or dressing up as a cow, or the next it could be gaining from the many learning opportunities through training courses for First Aid, food hygiene or manual handling or getting to grips with the new computer booking system. And how many jobs could you find yourself sweeping the floor or laying tables in the afternoon in preparation for an event and then rubbing shoulders in the evening with the First Minister at a Youth Burns Supper?!

It is these extremes, the busy madness and the calms before the storms that make working at the Dunblane Centre so interesting and fun. Uppermost though, is the fact that it is a customer-led business, with the aim of inclusion for all. As well as knowing that every individual who comes through the door is adding to its story, the staff must ensure that The Centre is attractive and welcoming to them all. There are always new people as well as the familiar faces to welcome and if by helping to keep The Centre a place where people want to be, then it will continue to offer many more special experiences and memories far into the future.

The Centre's Activities are organised by the Events Group, who are all volunteers, and **Rosie Mason** describes a little of what they do:

"The Events Group is made up of a loyal bunch of people, many of whom have been involved since the beginning. Not only do they turn up to meetings to organise the events but they often provide the raffle prizes, the home baking, set out the stalls, make the tea and clear up afterwards! Like all the other volunteers they not only help to make The Centre work but also secure its place as a valuable asset to the Dunblane community.

"I joined ten years ago. Since then the group has organised an enormous number of events and activities at The Centre, helping to raise much needed funds. The range has been pretty impressive from Burns Suppers to mad Comic Relief days, Funday Sundays, Nancy McLaren's race nights and hilarious comedy nights. The Robbie Williams tribute night was a particularly memorable one, in no small part due to Sally Weeks' cocktail mixing skills! Bingo Teas run like clockwork with people often seen staggering home laden with mops and buckets which they have won, stuffed with Nora Gilfillan's wonderful baking. And there's so much more."

There are Fun Days ...

.... and Play Days

There are Things to Buy ....

... or New Things to Try

Things to Eat ...

... and a Place to Meet

Parties and Dances ...

and Fitness Classes

Indoors ...

... Outdoors ...

and Many More Things We've Experienced over the Past Ten Years

Polling Days, Community Consultations, Fashion Shows, Scone Demonstrations, Jamming, Buggy Walking, Baby Sensory, Baby Massage, Gentle Body Conditioning/Recreation for Seniors, Dance School, Spinning, Circuits, Zumba, Roller Skating, Golf Lessons, Fencing, Basketball, Karate, Tae kwondo, LittleKicks, 5-a-side Football and Netball.

The Dunblane Centre has it all!

CHAPTER 7 – THE GIFT: A SHARED EXPERIENCE

Contributions from DUNBLANE and BEYOND

Monsignor Basil O'Sullivan, Church of the Holy Family

Raindrops on Roses and Whiskers on Kittens

The people who prepared the memorial service in the Cathedral wanted to celebrate the lives of Gwen and the children and at the same time point to a brighter future for the young people of Dunblane. So the theme of the service almost suggested itself: 'Out of Darkness into Light'. The well-known hymn 'Lead Kindly Light' was frequently sung in the Church of the Holy Family as it seemed to suit the mood of the Community at that particular time: "The night is dark and I am far from home; lead thou me on. Keep thou my feet; I do not ask to see the distant scene; one step enough for me".

It took rather more time for the idea of a community centre to develop and mature. It was hoped that the young people of Dunblane, and people not so young, would meet together, celebrate parties, join together in various projects and activities and in general enjoy themselves and each other. It took even more time and a great deal of hard work and generosity from many sources for The Centre to get off the ground and be the place that had been planned to help bring about that brighter future, for the darkness to lessen and the light to shine. On this Tenth Anniversary of its Opening we hope the light will continue to shine ever brighter in Dunblane for all its citizens, young and not so young, and that The Centre will continue to enjoy their whole-hearted support which it needs if it is to survive and thrive.

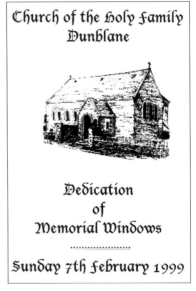

Church of the Holy Family
Dunblane

Dedication
of
Memorial Windows
....
Sunday 7th February 1999

A few of my favourite things –
long may they and the Dunblane Centre flourish.

Fiona Eadington, former Deputy Head of Dunblane Primary School

Over the last ten years, like many others I must have passed the Dunblane Centre several thousand times. Often there are banners telling of special events or wishing Andy "Good luck" or "Congratulations".

That is simply the tip of the iceberg. A look at the website gives an idea of all that goes on, and the wide range of ages involved.

On a personal note I regard The Centre as a testament to the generosity of spirit shown by those most deeply affected by the events of 13 March 1996. I am sure that some must have had reservations about the building of The Centre and it is to their credit that the project not only took off but has seen ten years of success. The Community owes a debt of gratitude to them and to those who so willingly gave their time and energy to ensure that The Centre came into being, and to those who have worked tirelessly during the last ten years to make the Dunblane Centre the success it is.

James Matthews, Sky News Journalist

Dunblane is threaded through my career as a journalist. Its present and its past, the best of times and the worst.

Today, the city provides a consistently good news story. Andy Murray.

When he's doing well, Sky News and other media film inside the Dunblane Centre and the global audience tunes into full-throated celebration at game, set and match to the Dunblane kid done good. It is 'Murraymania' at its most intense – the tension, noise, excitement and joy of a community that celebrates its hero and itself.

James Matthews reporting from The Centre on a memorable Day for Dunblane and British Sport.
(Picture: Sky News)

Through every tournament, every trophy and every roar from the floor, the Dunblane Centre has a calm constant. The seventeen of its citizens represented by images on its glass wall.

They are the people whose names I first learned amidst the grotesque unreality of March 1996. On a day when Dunblane, ashen-faced, led the international news. Seventeen names released in a media statement to accompany a black and white class photo. Many thousands of words have been written about the seventeen since.

Nothing, however, matches the story written by Dunblane itself.

Courage and dignity define the way in which the Community has rebuilt and grown through an enduring emotional struggle. There have been politics, too, and practical challenges confronted with strength, skill and success. The world that once looked on in horror has watched with admiration and respect as Dunblane continues to recover from its darkest day. In their name.

The city is a place shaped by its people and that includes the people it remembers at the Dunblane Centre.

Whatever the story we beam 'live' to the world from within its walls, there is no forgetting Victoria, Emma, Melissa, Charlotte, Kevin, Ross, David, Mhairi, Brett, Abigail, Gwen, Emily, Sophie, John, Joanna, Hannah and Megan. It is their story too.

Lynn Balman, DC Team Leader

My Fondest Memories

There are so many amazing memories I have from the Dunblane Centre and the people who support it, from Show in a Week (ALL of them) to Christmas Craft Fairs, Funday Sunday and working with all my favourite people, both volunteers and staff xx

But when asked to choose one for a piece in *The Wire*, a local community magazine, I decided that this had to be my most favourite, a 'Never Forget' memory .... Sunday 7 July 2013, **Wimbledon Men's Singles Final Day**.

We had shown and watched all of Andy's games leading up to the final, both staff and volunteers had sat and watched the semi-final whilst eating Chinese food at The Centre (no-one wanted to go home). When he won that match and we realised that Andy Murray had got to the final we were all very excited!!!

Wimbledon Men's Final Day – July 2013.

Not only was Dunblane buzzing with excitement, The Centre was electric with anticipation of the big day, with press, photographers and public phoning all the time wanting information of where they could watch the big final.

The Sunday morning was unusually busy, and once I opened The Centre I knew the day was going to be fabulous! And it was! We had Central FM here doing a

Dunblane celebrates Andy Murray's Victory.

live broadcast, along with what felt like every journalist from every newspaper as well as film crews from the BBC and Sky News. And from the minute we opened the doors (to a very large queue!) we knew we were going to have the most amazing day. The Centre was filled to its maximum, I was flying around the building doing interviews left, right and centre, helping people find seats, trying to control the number of people who could come in. There were people standing in doorways, on chairs, simply just anywhere to get a sense of the atmosphere of the place. They came from all over the country and beyond to be here in Dunblane. It was lovely listening to all the stories. I was doing interviews on television and radio, and I remember thinking this is a small taste of being a celebrity, because that's what Dunblane felt like, everyone wanting to be a part of it was incredible.

When Andy won there wasn't a dry eye in the building. I was standing on a chair (because I couldn't get a seat) close to the door crying my eyes out. Then I was very cruelly taken away to do an interview for Central FM and I will never forgive Steve Courtney for that because he has me on radio blubbing as I try to talk, and anyone who knows me knows I cry at anything. So it was very embarrassing, because the next day they kept playing my little interview all the time.

At the end I had a lovely lady give me a bottle of champagne to say thank you for the hospitality, which made me cry again. I had made a cake for the celebrations and this got demolished. Finally after everyone else had left, Andy's grandparents, Roy and Shirley Erskine, came by to say thank you for all the work we had done and how amazing the place looked on the television. I can quite honestly say that day was the most special to me and makes me very emotional (even typing this now).

The Wimbledon Final's Cake.

I feel very privileged to work at The Centre, there's not a day that goes by without me looking at the images on the windows and thinking about the children, a couple of whom I feel I miss like I knew them personally – I didn't. I know the beautiful families they left behind, I know them very well, and Pam & Kenny, Martyn & Barbara and Mick, I love them dearly – xxxxxx. Had The Centre not been built I would never have got to meet these very special and important people to me, four of whom were a huge part of my wedding day. I couldn't imagine the day without them.

Teresa McQuaid, DC Finance Assistant

I have worked at The Centre for the past four years and been a member almost from the beginning. I have always felt very welcome here.

I think it is a great place for the Dunblane community, especially for the young people, and wish it had been here when my children were young. It is a shame that it took such a terrible thing to happen to give us such a special place.

My 7-year-old nephew was over from Ireland last year and came down to play at The Centre. Now he keeps asking his mum when he'll be going back to Teresa's work!!

Louise Bleakley, DC Assistant

The Dunblane Centre is more than a building and a workplace to me, it's like being part of a very special and sometimes bonkers family. There is never a dull moment, which shows how much it has to offer to people from all parts of the Community. I have made some great friends through working there and have been a part of some new experiences, from seeing the madness of Show in a Week to helping with catering at a packed Burns Supper! It is a very special place and one which I hope to be involved with for a long time to come.

Nancy McLaren, Volunteer & Dunblane Youth Burns Club Founder & Organiser
Nancy's granddaughter Megan Turner was one of the victims in March 1996

I – The Joy of Volunteering

I had been in and out of The Centre for some weeks enjoying the chat of youthful workers and the noisy enthusiasm of the young. Standing in the office chatting to Scott, the first manager, I was taken aback when he said, "How about joining the fundraising committee?" This was a group of people who considered how we could raise finance for The Centre. They were all a lot younger than I was and very enthusiastic.

It was with trepidation that I agreed to join them on the understanding that I gave whatever time I could. Fundraising was what we wanted followed by good organisation once we decided on the event. I agreed to give it a try and I have never looked back. I enjoy the friendship of a young staff; I have the satisfaction of being needed, a great feeling when the years are passing quickly, and I have graduated to a desk job on a Monday! As an elderly volunteer I am delighted to have been accepted by a great bunch of people and sharing ideas for fundraising keeps me alert.

Nancy McLaren with Scotland's First Minister Alex Salmond at the Youth Burns Supper – January 2014.

I would encourage anyone to be a volunteer. You get a real sense of satisfaction and a bit of fun, something we all need in our lives. I am proud to know that I have put something into a very good cause and got so much back in return.

II - Race Night

Adults screaming at a 'jockey' hurriedly winding a piece of string around a wee stick of wood in order to get his horse (wooden on wheels) over the finish line does seem a bit childish, but great fun especially if your bet of £1 is liable to be a winner. The Race Night is a fun night for adults. Bring your own drink and nibbles and be prepared to bid for a horse and jockey. You might win the race and a bottle of wine.

Our Race Night is full of enthusiasm. "Don't forget to ask me next year" is a common request. We only need six sponsors, any offers? This Centre is for the Dunblane community to enjoy, irrespective of your age. Please make use of this wonderful facility. The Centre benefits greatly from these evenings as some of the proceeds go towards its upkeep.

III - The Show Must Go On

Uplifting and enthusiastic are words that come to mind when you see 100 young faces beaming at you from a stage and a tear comes to your eye as you share with them their pride and enthusiasm.

'The King and I' – Show in a Week 2013: (above) Full Cast; (l) Practising outside our Neighbours Marks & Spencer.

These young people are taking part in Show in a Week. That's all the preparation allowed and this surely encourages concentration! Words must be learned and strange tunes picked up, costumes chosen (what young person doesn't like dressing up?). The tiny tots are especially worth mentioning. They twirl and swirl in their lovely costumes, keeping an eye on the nearest 'big person' to ensure that they are doing the right thing at the right time and the 'big ones' usually are! Imagine what it is like encouraging 100 children to follow a routine! And of course they need to wave to Mum and Dad when they are singing! Could a star be born? What an opportunity they are given.

Matt Birnie, former Volunteer and DC Assistant

Being an assistant at the Dunblane Centre has got to have been my favourite job so far. The people and friends I met while working there made me look forward to going into work and enjoy being there. Some of the youth events we planned and organised were mad but provided some of the best memories by far.

The Centre Lock-ins were always a laugh. Trying to keep track of 50 kids for 12 hours overnight was a hard task but an enjoyable one. It was during these events that games such as computer chair basketball were created. By the time 7 am came around it was time for bacon butties and home. We were all knackered but high on sugar and caffeine and giggling uncontrollably.

The Beach Party was probably the event we put most work into and I think my favourite. Filling up one of our rooms with two tonnes of sand and having several paddling pools scattered both inside and outside had disaster written all over it. Three hours later we had covered the place in sand and water and completely used up The Centre's water supply. After we cleared what was left of the sand out of the Function Room it was time to sit down, enjoy some ice cream and discuss who to phone about the lack of running water in the building. Still makes me smile thinking about that situation.

The Beach Party.

Liz Kirkhope, former Pre-school Arts & Crafts Volunteer

As a mother first and foremost I started bringing my youngest son, Harvey, to pre-school Arts & Crafts on a Tuesday morning when he was 3 to 4 years old, not long after The Centre opened. We had so much fun and Harvey got so much out of the class that when he started Primary One at Dunblane Primary School I decided to volunteer as an Arts & Crafts tutor. I worked with Sue and Sheena and we all thoroughly enjoyed the pleasure we gave to so many pre-school children in Dunblane. I look back at my volunteering days at the Dunblane Centre with fond memories and wish them a very happy 10th Birthday.

Ali Hall, Pre-school Arts & Crafts Volunteer

I discovered the Dunblane Centre when my kids were tiny and was delighted to find the Sports Hall was available and hugely appreciated that it provided a large indoor play space where the older one could RUN (especially when it was raining outside) and the wee one could explore on the soft play mats. Even better was realising we could go up and eat a packed lunch and use the tuck shop for treats and a coffee for me in a relaxed kiddie-friendly environment – with play corner! What more could you want? I soon became a volunteer at The Centre, doing one of the pre-school art classes which I and my children continue to enjoy.

Val Storrie, Spanish Teacher

I began using The Centre in 2006 when I set up a small business running fun Spanish classes for children and adults in the area. The facilities are first class and the parents can wait in the reception area with their younger kids and play with the toys, read or watch TV. Children waiting to go into the classes can play table tennis or use the computer.

The staff are so welcoming and helpful, and despite The Centre being my workplace it certainly feels a lot more than that – it is warm, welcoming and the heart of the Community. Even my four kids, the crazy gang, are welcome there and my husband uses The Centre every Friday for football.

I feel so very privileged to be a small part of The Centre and I know that it will play an important role in my kids' lives growing up in Dunblane.

Rosemarie Laird, German Teacher and The Centre's most Senior Volunteer

Volunteering

Why? – The Dunblane Centre is a charity and relies on volunteers to remain viable. Thankfully there is a strong brigade of hard working helpers coming and going with lots of different talents, all leading to great success. Congratulations on your Tenth Anniversary.

Every volunteer has his or her own story to tell about why they feel compelled to help. My story goes back to childhood and teenage years, experiencing war time with painful interruption of our happy family life, distractions to the point of losing every basic necessity required for life and starvation lasting until three years after the end of World War II. I was still at school when we got nourishing soups from Sweden and America. I vowed then that one day I would give back to the community what we had received when we were in dire need of help.

When? Where? – Years passed before the opportunities came my way to keep my vow. My first years as a volunteer started in a newly opened charity shop for Cancer Research. Home and work commitments did not give me much spare time to do this. And then in 1992, I was retired by then, I met Magnus MacFarlane Barrow in Dalmally. He was involved in collecting goods and food for people in war-torn Bosnia and transported the donations in a Jeep or Transit Van and later by lorry. This was a real inspiration to me and I responded by running a charity shop which he opened in Dunblane.

When my physical strength was unable to stand up any longer to the demands n the shop I had to stop volunteering. What else could I do? Learning that Spanish lessons were being taught at the Dunblane Centre I had the idea that there might be some interest in Beginners German lessons. As I have no formal teaching training I was unsure if I had the skills required to teach my native German language. Would I overcome the initial fear and insecurity? I looked into it and decided to give it a try. I am happy to say I enjoy having taken this step some years ago and could continue keeping the vow I made as a teenager.

Jenny Morton, Volunteer

My younger sister Emily was one of the children who lost her life at Dunblane Primary School in 1996. As a result of this I was part of a small group of children who attended the Abbey Road Studios to record 'Knockin' on Heaven's Door' with Ted Christopher (see Chapter 5). I remember it being an incredibly emotional time as we were still struggling with what had happened in Dunblane. However, there was something very comforting about uniting for such an important cause and paying tribute to Gwen and the children. Our song eventually went to number 1 and I feel extremely proud of what it helped to achieve.

*Jenny Morton
(l) helping at Halloween.*

As I have always enjoyed working with children and felt closely connected to the Dunblane Centre I began volunteering at the Youth Clubs in 2010.

The Centre is a lovely place which regularly brings the Community together and commemorates Gwen and the children beautifully. I have developed great and lasting friendships with the staff, youth workers and volunteers who have helped me in so many ways over the years. It's especially nice to see the entertainment and joy it provides for the children attending the clubs, and I believe it is a place my sister and her friends would have loved.

Jeannie Gray, DC Youth Worker

I started working at The Centre in April 2011. Before I began I didn't know The Centre was there – I was not from Dunblane. However, from the moment I stepped inside the building I was amazed by how important it was. The detail there is so very special. I am honoured that I have been able to be part of such a unique place and have been very lucky to get to know the young people of Dunblane and give them the opportunity to access this amazing facility. I have met some truly remarkable people through working at The Centre and I hope that we can continue to serve the Community for another ten years. It is a very beautiful legacy.

Phyllis Dewar, Fitness Instructor

I have worked as a fitness instructor at the Dunblane Centre since it opened in September 2004. I was here with my hard hat deciding how many step boards we could fit into the Fitness Studio. We offer classes to suit everyone no matter how fit or unfit they think they are. In the mornings we provide a crèche, and the children can be so funny copying us from the windows above with their little flashing lights on their shoes. Class members are very friendly, all having a good chat before we start, so everyone has a smile on their face. I love working at The Centre and always look forward to meeting new members. I feel great to see members getting results and enjoying the classes. I get lots of satisfaction from teaching and lots of laughs.

Janet McClelland [Hally], Volunteer and Former Fitness Instructor

The Centre helped me to gain confidence to start as a volunteer. From there it supported me and allowed me to take on more classes. I started studying again. I moved from being a person who had long term mental health problems to being able to run my own business. The people have made the building into a very special place for everyone and especially for me.

Maria Hybszer, Pilates Instructor

I've been teaching Pilates at The Centre for a while now and really enjoy coming every Tuesday and Thursday. Everyone has always been very welcoming and appreciative of my efforts.

I love working there and seeing how Pilates is helping the participants to feel good in themselves and seeing their bodies changing for the better. I think you all do a marvellous job. The Centre has such a lot going for it and I wish you all the very best for the next ten years.

Jill Hall, Volunteer

I became involved in The Centre a few weeks before the Opening in 2004. There was much to do, furnishing, helping on the day, snagging. After opening it took a while for The Centre to find its feet, a lot of thinking and energy went into working out how best to operate, serve the Community and survive. I watched a small team of generous, community-minded individuals grow in number, ability and strength. For me, it was satisfying, fun and gave me the chance to learn much more about the community in Dunblane.

Following a 6-year absence living abroad I am again using The Centre. It is great to see how its role in the Community is growing and to see a broad range of people involved in running and using this very special facility. I'm very glad it's there.

Bridget McCalister, Volunteer, Dunblane Centre Gardens

I have looked after the beds round the car park and behind the Art Room for the last nine years, with the help of a band of friends – at present Lynne and Iona.

When we started a lot of the hedge was dead, the soil was full of rubble and the beds were full of weeds, ivy and a few institutional shrubs put in by the builders. Over the years we have dug in tons of compost and spread even more bark chippings, replanted the hedges and put in loads of bulbs and perennial plants into the borders. The latter were all donated by local people.

Mind you, after about five years of doing this Tom and Gwen, an elderly couple who played table tennis at The Centre every week, seeing us enter with muddy hands and clothes and being told we were the gardeners asked "Where is the garden?" That made me smile so I hope that after ten years it is more obvious where the garden is!

Plans are now in place for an orchard and extension of the wild flower meadow which will be a lovely 10-year project and should give pleasure for years to come.

The gardeners get great delight watching the garden as we drive and walk by. We would love new members of the team, and donations of perennials, so please get in touch if you can help.

The Cheerful Childminders' Group

We as a group have been using the facilities twice a week for our child-minded children for 10 years since it opened. In fact we had booked our space before the Grand Opening! The childminders enjoy meeting up for a chat and a cuppa. The children enjoy playing together in a safe and happy environment. We hope to continue using The Centre for the next ten years!!!

James Parker, former Volunteer and DC Assistant

I was involved with The Centre for a good few years back in the early days, just as it was opening. What I always remember is the fun times working there, whether it was a quick bounce on the bouncy castle before putting it away or a Youth Club all-nighter. Then there was the general banter that we used to have as a team. One of my funniest, albeit embarrassing, memories was from a time just before The Centre opened. I was trying to get the air conditioning on and was sitting behind the front desk looking for buttons. After a couple of minutes searching I found these two red buttons on the desk and in my young naivety thought they must control the aircon. Five minutes later the police turned up, apparently I'd pressed the emergency alarm! Luckily everyone saw the funny side of it – as the system had never been tested my mistake was seen as a good test!

The Centre was always about the Community and giving young people an advantage in Dunblane. For me this was providing the chance to gain valuable experience in IT. I'm extremely grateful for the degree of patience people must have had for me, especially early on. Through volunteering there, I had the chance to work with a wide variety of people and learn new skills – dealing with people

James Parker with Maureen Simpson.

when bookings went wrong and adding that little extra that improves someone's experience. The underlying skills gave me an advantage in my work today, although I've yet to be asked to put away a bouncy castle again (I do still remember how!).

Martyn Dunn, DC Trustee

The tragic loss of our daughter Charlotte on 13 March 1996 was the worst moment in my life. Since then we have survived and moved on with the memory of Charlotte and her friends always with us.

When in 2011 I was made redundant, the process involved and the pressure of the new job I'd been fortunate to find resulted in a severe bout of depression and I had to spend some time away in hospital. These events made me review my life, and in August 2012 I decided to give up work and take some time out to sort myself out and plan my life going forward.

Although I had attended the Grand Opening and been to other events, I had never made The Centre a part of my life. I felt it didn't offer me the things that would help me move on with my life. My wife Barbara, however, was going to fitness classes and had become a volunteer, offering help with a friend at two Friday morning pre-school art classes.

When, on one of those Fridays, her friend couldn't make the class Barbara asked me to come along to help. I found that I really enjoyed myself and got a great feeling assisting the children and seeing them having fun. I continued to help out when needed, and during these sessions I began to spot a few odd jobs that required attention. My background was in engineering and I realised I could offer relevant experience and my services. Friday mornings at The Centre became a regular fixture in my diary, helping out with art classes, doing odd jobs and organising contractors to carry out regular repairs and service main plant items.

When in August 2013 I decided to return to work, I wanted the time needed to carry on with my volunteering because of the great pleasure it had given me. Fortunately I found an employer who was open to my working a 4-day week. And I was delighted to increase my involvement at The Centre after being asked by the Board whether I would like to become a trustee with responsibility for facilities management. I agreed.

After a long period of uncertainty about what The Centre could offer me I can now see that my involvement in its life provided a key turning point in my recovery and return to work. I have a happy life/work balance and relish being involved in two of the Tenth Anniversary projects (The Garden and The Refurbishment) (see Chapter 8). It is a pleasure to be helping support The Centre's great activities and make it a special place for the local community to enjoy. Let's keep it going!

Gemma Beher, DC Trustee

I first heard about the Dunblane Centre when I was searching the net trying to predict what kind of new life I would have once I moved to the town in 2004. I was dreading the move – pregnant with number one son, I'd just left a very cushy job at Uni and was not happy about leaving behind friends and stability in Durham, but I had to find out what was on offer 'up there'. It felt like the back of beyond to me and I was really mad with my husband for chasing a promotion so badly that we had to uproot.

Yet ten years down the line, two children, several hundred fitness classes, too many Bingo Teas and umpteen raffles later I am proud to be involved with The Centre and all that it is. It has been a place to go and park my pregnant belly on comfy sofas while chatting to all the people who passed through its doors and who I can now call friends. Scott Neil, the manager back then, effortlessly roped me into running a children's art class with a smile and some flattery, which had me covered in PVA and glitter in no time at all. I have lost count of the number of times I have swept the Sports Hall following some event or other, only to return a day or so later to find it covered in the mud off the boots of the 5-a-side team, but I can smile at that knowing that so many people use it every day for all sorts of reasons. The Centre to me has been a place of friendship, compassion and support; a place of blood, sweat and tears (otherwise known as fitness classes); somewhere that I can pop into for a quick natter (or cry if the mood takes me) while I wait to collect the children from activities.

It means so much to me that The Centre is there for the people of Dunblane; I couldn't have settled so well without it. For all that it is, for all the generosity of spirit and creativity housed within its walls, I am incredibly grateful.

Howard Barr, DC Treasurer

A Recent Trustee's Perspective

It was during 2012 that Steve Birnie first hinted at the prospect of me becoming involved with The Centre. I had been introduced to Steve some months previously in my capacity as a financial planner, and his enthusiasm for The Centre and all those involved soon became apparent. It appeared that The Centre was going through a period of personnel change, and the need for a treasurer was becoming acute. I remember attending the first trustees' meeting and being hugely impressed with the commitment shown by the Board. But owing to the economic conditions prevalent at that point The Centre was navigating a difficult financial period.

Thus, I agreed to take on the position and it seemed only natural to become a full trustee and bring the few skills I had to the group. Those first few months saw me coming to know the staff, volunteers and other trustees, and I soon felt at home and that I could contribute not only some financial acumen but also a general business overview.

What followed was somewhat unexpected! As a moderately keen cyclist I had a vague notion of celebrating my 50th year with a challenge, primarily to prove to myself that I wasn't yet entirely over the hill. So, after some deliberation, I decided to join a group which planned to cycle from Land's End to John O' Groats over a nine day period in September 2013. I'd had some experience of a similar type of challenge cycling from London to Paris in 2011 but realised that LEJOG was an altogether tougher proposition, covering an average of 110 miles a day for nine days without a break.

So, in order to ensure I couldn't back out, I suggested to the trustees that it might present an opportunity to raise some funds for The Centre, along with a degree of publicity. Come May 2013 I embarked on a recommended training schedule which would see me cover gradually increasing mileages over the summer, thankfully a relatively dry one as far as Scottish summers go. The target was to get between 2,500 and 3,000 miles into my legs by the end of August and to raise a minimum of £3,500.

(l & centre) Howard Barr at The Centre; (r) Howard's Way.

Over that period I not only acquired a new LYCRA wardrobe but shed two stones resulting in me needing a new regular wardrobe too! Soon enough, the trip loomed and I set off with bike and hire car to Penzance to start my adventure.

I described the next gruelling nine days in a blog. I had some great memories with some of the most genuine and sincere people you could hope to meet and raised £4,000 for a very worthwhile cause, The Centre – way beyond my expectations and all down to the generosity of family, friends and clients. A recreational 50-year-old wannabe cyclist can't ask for much more than that.

I continue to be amazed at the community spirit demonstrated by so many who regard The Centre as their own and feel privileged to play a continuing small part in so worthwhile a cause.

Dave Spooner, DC Trustee

Dunblane Centre for me distils all that is good in a community – energy, challenge, inspiration, laughter, tears, sharing, believing, supporting, giving, receiving, celebrating, remembrance, hope and pride. Each time I walk in I feel connected to all these things and everyone past and present that makes it so, and I am so grateful.

Sue Lockwood, former DC Trustee and Events Committee Volunteer

Growing up in Dunblane was special to me. Moving back here with our family just as the Dunblane Centre was about to open, I knew that I wanted to help out as a volunteer. As a parent, I felt it was the least I could do.

The Dunblane Centre is a unique facility – it is here as a living memorial and as a gift to the entire community. Over the last decade I have enjoyed working along-side friends old and new in a variety of ways. It has been very rewarding and it is good to know that our help makes a difference. I just can't quite believe we've been doing it for ten years already!

Jim Cattan, former DC Chairman

Jim was a member of Dunblane Primary School Board at the time of the Tragedy so was involved from the beginning, in the early days at the Youth Drop-in in the TA Building, during the time when the Youth Project was housed in a unit on the Duckburn Industrial Estate and then throughout the building of The Centre. He was a trustee, a director and lead signatory for the Disclosures of all involved with The Centre.

"13 March 1996 was a dark time for Dunblane and our thoughts are with everybody affected by the tragedy. The worst possible events in life often bring out the best in people, and we hope that the Dunblane Centre is a great example of how this community continues to pull together and look to the future. Designed for present and future generations, it is already a living, breathing integral part of Dunblane.

Jim Cattan cutting The Centre's 5th Anniversary Cake.

"The Dunblane Centre could not function without the tireless efforts of many volunteers who contribute their time, skills and resources. It is the dedicated staff and this community which makes The Centre what it is."

Sandra Gault, Member

I attend fitness classes four times a week at the Dunblane Centre. It is an excellent resource shared by people from both the town and the surrounding district. It gives the children of Dunblane a wide range of engaging activities, especially in the school holidays, as well as providing informal gatherings in the evenings. We are very fortunate in having many dedicated volunteer staff to assist the permanent staff in making all this possible. Good luck for the next ten years.

Nicky Farthing, Member

For the last ten years, the Dunblane Centre has been a regular part of our family's lives.

As a busy Mum, I really enjoy the fitness classes. Being right in Dunblane, The Centre is easily accessible, which is important when time is precious. And I have to admit, it's not just for getting fit, but for the social aspect of it too! I've made many good friends over the years whom I wouldn't have met otherwise. We usually grab a coffee after class, which is a great excuse for a girly gossip – putting the world to rights, of course, and making plans for our fun nights out – a birthday celebration being a great excuse for a glass of Vino!

The Centre has been great for, and well used, by both of my children, who have enjoyed various activities there over the years. Being able to use The Centre to host birthday parties is a real plus for parents. The facilities are excellent, and there's lots of space for children to run around and have fun! One of my boys had a football themed party there, which is not the kind of party you'd be able to hold in the sitting room at home! A professional personality 'did the honours', much to the delight of the children in attendance, and he was so impressed by the place that he signed some balls to be raffled for Dunblane Centre funds.

Fitness Ladies including Nicky Farthing (2nd right) and Instructor Phyllis Dewar (3rd left).

Now they are both growing up fast, the Youth Club has been excellent for them socially and my younger son is now volunteering there as part of his Duke of Edinburgh Award.

Long may the wonderful facilities and huge range of available activities keep The Centre as such a treasured 'heart' of our community.

Gina Nevill, User and Performer

The Dunblane Centre shows have been a huge part of my childhood. I have grown up with them since I was five and have loved every minute. I remember crying at the end of 'Wizard of Oz' when I was nine because it was over and I'd had such a great time, feeling very mature because I was crying for both happy and sad reasons. When I look on it now it's quite embarrassing and funny! Five years later, when I was 13, I was in the same position at the end of the 'Show of Shows', though this time I was sobbing a lot harder. I don't know

Gina Nevill (in the Red Hat) and the Cast of 'Fame'.

how to describe the emotion I felt but it was one of the best. These shows have been amazing and I love them so much so "Thank You Pamela and the Dunblane Centre. Happy 10th Birthday"!

...and her mum Harriet Nevill, User and Show Choir Member

The Centre plays a constant part of our annual life as a family. From the first 'Show in a Week' which has now become a fixture of the summer – costume preparation and adaptation, line-learning, new songs and general excitement building up to the shows – to autumn Sundays and the Panto rehearsals. The girls love it all and have met some lovely people along the way. And now there is the Show Choir – a weekly get together for singing, tea and cake and my own chance for harmonies and performances.

What Some Other Younger Users Say

Euan Nicol – The Dunblane Centre to me is a place to come and chill and have a laugh with my friends. The youth workers are all chilled and good to be about. It's a great place, it's full of things for us to do and a relaxed place to be.

Ruairdh Thomson – I enjoy coming down to The Centre because of the staff. The staff are funny and you can have a laugh with them. My favourite thing is the Saturday Night Project because you get to play football and Xbox and hang out with your friends.

Ruairdh Thomson, Callum McIntosh and Euan Nicol,

Callum McIntosh – What I like about the Centre is the Saturday Night Project as this is the main relationship we have with the staff, there are always fun things on and it's a great place to be.

Angus Clelland – Good youth workers who you can have a conversation with and the place has a warm atmosphere.

Alan Nichols, who runs the Sports First Aid Training for all The Centre's Staff, writes a Personal Timeline (Alan was also an original member of the Dunblane First Responders).

In September 1989 I accepted an appointment at the University of Stirling and soon decided that Dunblane would provide a comfortable community into which my family could follow me from our previous home in Belfast. Everyone quickly became involved with local schools, scouting and community activities. My work-place interests in sports provision and fundraising brought queries regarding the development of Dunblane's sports facilities. In particular costings for the possible construction of a local swimming pool were high on the agenda.

All of these thoughts were overwhelmed by the terrible events of 13 March 1996. Everyone will have their personal and shared emotions, a personal re-collection for me being the immense sympathy expressed by erstwhile colleagues throughout the island of Ireland. Despite their own tragic circumstances at that time, a stream of donations and condolences ensued.

There followed a period of adjustment. The volume of donations received following the Tragedy, and the self-evident need to make positive use of such goodwill, led to the nascent youth club in the Duckburn Industrial Estate and the developments, described in detail earlier in this book, which led to the planning and construction of the Dunblane Centre. We sought an appropriate memorial to reflect the sentiments and interests of the entire community.

Perhaps my experience would be useful in this aspect of planning? My personal thoughts suggested a wide choice of sporting and fitness activities. These

should be appropriately equipped and staffed, designed to accommodate all levels of performance and all age groups. There should be support from the governing bodies of sport where appropriate. However, with funding already committed to meet building costs, further fundraising would be essential for the provision of sports equipment. Catalogues were consulted and funding sources approached. In order to establish the widest assortment of activities, equipment was to be provided for sports ranging alphabetically from badminton to yoga! A typical recollection from this time is of meeting the local golf club committee to plead for equipment funding. We were asked to wait outside the committee room whilst our request was discussed and then invited back. Only one question was raised, "Had we asked for enough?"

An interesting development has been the welfare focus, in which the health benefits of exercise have remained an underlying feature of our exercise programme. Coincidentally staff training has always included specialist consideration of sports injuries – the initial courses provided the foundation for what has now become a nationally accredited award. Since 2009 The Centre has also provided the training location for Dunblane's First Response emergency ambulance charity (see Chapter 9).

Has the Dunblane Centre achieved its original community objectives? The levels of innovation and activity are undoubtedly higher than anticipated and typical problems which might have arisen from the range of client groups served are fewer than anticipated. There may be less competitive sport than expected, perhaps because there are few local leagues or qualification courses, but the fashions of fitness have remained a recurrent and popular theme throughout the decade. Most vitally, throughout its first decade the programme has been consistently responsive and innovative.

From my personal perspective, the Dunblane Centre remains highly successful, serving all sectors of the community with a popular programme. Thank you everyone.

Paul Christmas, Captain 25th Stirling (Dunblane) Company, The Boys' Brigade

The BB Annual Display at The Centre.

The Dunblane Centre is a terrific and much-valued community facility which the Boys' Brigade in Dunblane uses on a regular basis for both local events such as table tennis and other sports and national competitions which include 5-a-side football for both Junior and Senior boys, badminton and basketball. We also hold our annual display in the Sports Hall every May as it is the only location in Dunblane big enough to hold all 185 boys and their parents, friends and supporters!

Our recent 2014 Annual Display saw more than 450 people in the facility.

The Centre staff are always fantastic in their attitude and willingness to accommodate what can be a bunch of competitive, noisy boys!

The BB views the Dunblane Centre as a cherished, well-run and indispensable community resource and we are very grateful to everyone there who looks after us.

Simon Fraser, Community PC

I had the pleasure of being the community police officer in Dunblane for over 7 years and throughout that time I spent many happy hours at the Dunblane Centre. Every time I was there I was made to feel so welcome by staff/visitors alike – sometimes it was easy to forget I was actually working.

I had involvement at The Centre on numerous fronts. I used to hold a monthly community surgery which to everyone's surprise actually had people visit and was well received. I was heavily involved with youth work at The Centre and had a great relationship with three youth workers, Bob, Jeannie and latterly Andy, during my time in Dunblane. They are a credit to The Centre and the youth work that is carried out, a great assistance to me as well as a huge benefit to the town's young people. The Saturday Night Project which is currently running at The Centre allows youngsters to spend time on a Saturday night in a safe environment.

I was asked to attend a number of the Funday Sunday events and I am not sure who enjoyed these more, me or the local community who got the chance to throw wet sponges at me! It was always a great event and it was nice to be able to contribute to the fundraising.

I always enjoyed meeting and working with the staff at The Centre, the trustees and the volunteers. I worked with three managers during my time in Dunblane from Scott, who never made it common knowledge that he lost money to me on the golf course, to the current manager Gemma who as well as being a credit to The Centre is mad as a hatter.

One other person I feel I should mention is Pamela Mackie. During seven years I think I could count on the fingers of one hand the number of times I was in the Centre and she was not there. I am sure she would be as well moving in given the amount of time she spends there.

I have a story about one of the staff, young Joe, who on passing his test got a new car with a private number plate. I was in one evening not long after he got the car and he was not slow in telling me about it. I said that was a coincidence as I had received some calls about his vehicle and the manner of the driving and that I would need a private word with him. I was only winding him up but his face was a picture. I left shortly after that and to this day I have never told him I was kidding. I am sure he will have worked it out by now.

I have many great memories of time spent at the Dunblane Centre and was fortunate in my role as the community police officer to have a place that was not only welcoming but also a great assistance to my job. It is an excellent community facility and I hope that it continues to flourish for the next ten years and many years after that.

I am no longer working in Dunblane and miss my regular visits and obligatory coffee at The Centre but hopefully will be back on a regular basis.

And Finally, the Thoughts of Lesley Shaw, DC Manager from 2009 to 2012

First of all, congratulations to everyone who has been involved with the Dunblane Centre over the years – who have all, in one way or another contributed to it completing its first decade; it really is quite an achievement!

I took great pride in my time as Centre Manager and still do. To be invited into The Centre's 'Family' and trusted to run such a unique and important place is something that I will always treasure.

Managing any organisation has its challenges and my time was no different. However, what I took most from my time at The Centre was the opportunity to

meet and get to know the people behind the project and who brought it to life; those who continue to keep its heart pumping with fundraisers, events and ideas to drive it forward. The challenges to get The Centre to where it is today and to sustain its future have required great determination and passion from all involved, and it is important to understand what it represents within the Community and to those families for whom it's not just a youth and community centre but a legacy for their family.

Listening to these stories is what made The Centre so important to me and my drive to want to do a 'good job'.

The experience went so far as to make me re-think my career and realise that, as important as business is, I am more interested in the people and stories behind it. Consequently, I am now re-training as a counsellor to engage with people and their stories more directly. I am so grateful for my time at The Centre in helping me recognise that and for the opportunity to help others.

CHAPTER 8 – CELEBRATING OUR TENTH YEAR

PAM ROSS, NORA GILFILLAN and MICK NORTH
with contributions from SIMON THOMAS, NANCY McLAREN, JO BICHENO, WALTER BAILEY and LEIGH AUSTIN

The Centre's Tenth Year is accompanied by many important events – some are already annual features in The Centre's calendar, others were planned specifically for our special year. This chapter allows us to share some of those celebrations.

Funday Sunday – Coinciding with The Centre's birthday each September, Funday Sunday is, as the name tells you, a day devoted to fun, and one especially for kids. Funday Sunday 2014 is still to come and to mark a special birthday this will be a massive celebratory event for the entire community to enjoy as a 'thank you' for the commitment and support over the last ten years. You can get a flavour of Funday Sundays in Chapters 5 and 6.

Tartan Ball – Dancing to the Soul Doctors – November 2013.

Tartan Ball – A fundraising dinner-dance was held at the Stirling University Management Centre with music provided by our favourite 10 piece blues and soul band, The Soul Doctors. The black tie event raised nearly £4,000 for The Centre. A fundraising ball will now become an annual event and the next one in November 2014, held at Dunblane Hydro, will be a fitting climax to the Anniversary Celebrations.

The Soul Doctors' **Simon Thomas** adds:

"The Soul Doctors were kindly asked to play at the Dunblane Centre a few years ago, and have had the pleasure of returning on more than one occasion. We are always given a very warm welcome, and now regard ourselves as The Centre's 'House Band'. A few of us have been involved in a number of the dramatic productions and have great affection for The Centre. We are especially looking forward to playing at the St Andrew's Night fundraiser, and can honestly say the group of people we meet and deal with when in Dunblane

are some of the nicest we play for, with a great atmosphere. We hope we can continue our association for many more years to come"!

Youth Burns Night Supper – Each January the Dunblane Centre Youth Burns Club organises a Burns Night Supper. The guests are treated to performances from many of its young members. The Toast to the Lassies is led by the Head Boy of Dunblane High School and the Head Girl makes The Reply. Though not specifically part of the Tenth Anniversary celebrations, the 2014 Supper was very much in keeping with our important year with special guest Alex Salmond, Scotland's First Minister, delivering the Immortal Memory. The event was celebrated on the front page of The Robert Burns World Federation Newsletter which described how:

"Twenty young local artists entertained the company with superbly delivered speeches, music, recitation and songs. Rt Hon Alex Salmond delivered a humorous and informative Immortal Memory."

The Youth Burns Night Supper – January 2014. (Clockwise from the top): Alex Salmond delivers the Immortal Memory with Stewart Prodger (trustee) and Jennifer Steen (chair), The First Minister with Piper Evan Raymond; Performers and Guests before the Supper; Top Table Guests singing Auld Lang Syne; Holly Jarvis addressing the Haggis.

104

Organiser **Nancy McLaren** writes:

"Confidence and assurance are what you are aware of as you watch the young person perform. These words are seldom used but this is what hits you when the Burns Supper takes place. Twenty young people aged 10-17 entertain 90 adults and we can only sing their praises, an occasion for feeling pride.

"These young people have recognised the benefits of rehearsal and have been rewarded. They have all the abilities you need for entertaining, and as their tutor I am proud that our joint ideas have been put to the test and the entertainers have been successful beyond belief. To reinforce this comment they took part in the Perth Burns School Festival and won four lovely silver cups.

"No other youth club encourages public speaking, but without a doubt these boys and girls gain confidence. As one young girl remarked "I was terrified at the beginning but when I finished I felt great". How is that for a thank you?"

The haggis for the annual Burns Supper is supplied by local butcher John Hill and no Dunblane Centre raffle would be complete without a John Hill steak pie! Persuaded by Les Morton to become involved, John helped The Centre's youngsters during the early days by providing disco music in the Function Room on Tuesdays and Thursdays. He also fondly remembers a special New Year's Day Party for friends and families at the Centre in 2005 when there was music and a meal for 150 people. It was a day where everyone mucked in and had a brilliant day, and it's still talked about yet!

Show of Shows – Coordinated by Pamela Mackie and the team, the Show of Shows reprised all the shows held over the previous nine years: Show in a Week, Concerts, Pantos – EVERYTHING! It was a fantastic event which showcased the musical talent Dunblane has to offer! There is much more about The Centre's Shows in Chapter 6.

Show of Shows –
March 2014.
(l) Rehearsals and (bottom)
All Night Preparations in
the Sports Hall.

SHOW OF SHOWS

celebrating 10 years of
performing arts at the
Dunblane Centre

21st and 22nd March 2014
7.30pm / 2pm matinee
Tickets £8 full £5 conc from the Dunblane Centre
01786824224 or online www.theatreindunblane.co.uk

Panto – another of The Centre's annual events.

In 2013 it was

'Sleeping Beauty': Rehearsals and Production

Show in a Week – August 2014 – As we completed this book the planning for 'Oliver' was over and rehearsals had begun.

The Tepee Community Project – explained by Jo Bicheno

This project got off the ground when Nora sent me a wonderful photo of a knitted tepee that she'd spotted on the internet. After thinking and chatting about it, we thought it would be a perfect project to mark the Tenth Anniversary of The Centre: making something to last, which people of all ages could see and enjoy and which hopefully, in its making, would involve as many people from the community of Dunblane as possible.

It has turned into a very inspiring and fun project for all involved. We started the knitting group at The Centre on a Thursday evening and put out the word that all were welcome, whatever the level of their knitting or crocheting skills! Old friends and new have turned up – aged from days old (though he didn't do much knitting!) to their 80s and the group has grown larger and larger each week as more people hear about the tepee and want to get involved. To date over 60 people have taken part. Some, who had hardly knitted in their lives, are now experts, experienced knitters and crocheters have passed on their skills and of course the highlights of the evenings have been the chats, the community spirit and the cups of tea. Others who couldn't manage along have knitted at home and we've had lots of welcome donations of wool. The only rule has been that the squares should measure 8 x 8 inches and it's been surprising and amazing to see the variety of colours and patterns, some even works of art, as the squares have piled up at The Centre.

By the end of June we had almost 700 squares and the task for July and August (perhaps the biggest challenge of all!) was to assemble the squares into a tepee shape and fit them onto the frame. Certainly the tepee will be a bright and wonderful symbol of Dunblane's community spirit and hopefully a fun place to play for some time to come! And happily the group too seems likely to be here for some time to come: it's been such a success that we hope to continue meeting, knitting and chatting, long after the tepee has been completed.

Tree of Life - A permanent legacy from the Tenth Anniversary celebrations is going to be a wooden sculpture to be installed in the

(above) Two of The Centre's 'Tree of Life' Group, Nora Gilfillan and Pam Ross, with artist Walter Bailey in April 2014; (l) Pam and Nora discuss the Carpet for The Centre's Entrance.

entrance of The Centre. The 'Tree of Life' is being made by Walter Bailey who sculpted 'The Flame for Dunblane' as a memorial to the Dunblane victims (see Chapter 2). Those who have been key contributors to the creation and life of The Centre will be recognised in a way that is an integral part of the design of the Tree. Michelle Scobbie, one of the Tree of Life group, has been training to teach yoga and ran sessions in her own time at the Centre on a Saturday. The £500 she received in class fees during this time was very kindly donated towards this special project for which we are most grateful.

Walter Bailey adds his own thoughts:

"'The Tree of Life' celebrates the Dunblane Centre, the vital living hub of a healing community.

"The sculpture is a two meter wide wall-mounted relief carving in redwood, carved with a chainsaw and chisels, scorched by fire, then worked by hand to reveal the striking wood grain.

Walter's Initial Design.

Walter working on the Sculpture.

"Motifs of leaves and flames are cut right through the sculpture allowing light to come through. Seventeen pale blue flames are held within the branches, tenderly celebrating the lives of the sixteen children and their teacher lost on March 13th 1996. Leaf motifs reveal the names of some of the generous people whose work and support have contributed to the success of The Centre.

"With the 'Tree of Life' I wanted to honour the work of the many people who have given so much in order to create the thriving community that is the Dunblane Centre, and it is an honour for me to have taken on the commision for the 'Tree of Life'".

The Big Youthie – As a Centre focused around young people, we wanted to have a year of youth events through which they can celebrate ten years in their own personal way.

DC Assistant Leigh Austin describes one of The Big Youthie's Celebratory Events

'Unleash the Brick' forms part of the Big Youthie programme and like many things at The Centre, it grew from a simple idea. Back in 2013 a suggestion was made about building a large model out of LEGO for the celebrations and inviting young people along to help construct it. This suggestion turned into an event and

consequently a committee was set up to oversee it. Knowing of my general love for all things LEGO I was 'volunteered' onto the committee. By the time the committee had met again I had somehow, and I'm really not entirely sure how, been placed in charge.

"Many discussions ensued about what to build. A model of The Centre? Dunblane Cathedral? The Andy Murray golden postbox? The more we discussed things the more ridiculous our suggestions became. If we had been allowed to continue, I swear the Sports Hall would have been taken over by a scale model of the city itself. Eventually, however, cost reined in our ideas; LEGO is not a cheap medium from which to build things. We settled not for a 3D model but rather a 2D mosaic of Dunblane's greatest hero, Andy Murray. Negotiations with Bright Bricks, a LEGO building company in England, began and they turned our photo into a design for a 2.0m x 1.5m mosaic!

But what turned this mosaic building event into the beast that is now 'Unleash The Brick'? Personally I blame Google. As I spent hours searching online for different LEGO models I came across more and more things that people had done with these little plastic bricks: from catapults and earthquake proof models to bracelets, key rings and even LEGO being used to paint pictures. As I explained these ideas to the committee we started to wonder if we could run some of these activities alongside the mosaic build. A proposal was put to the trustees to allow us to spend a little more money to help the event and, thankfully, their approval meant we could begin planning on a larger scale.

The mosaic has been ordered, and remains at the heart of 'Unleash the Brick'. But it has now been assimilated into a bigger event rather than being the event itself. We currently have 14 confirmed activities for the day including big screen LEGO video games, a chance to meet LEGO Batman, a challenge zone comprising various science and engineering based tasks and a create zone, for all things art and crafty! As each day goes by another suggestion pops up into my Facebook news feed as to what we could do, and I go "yep, let's do it!". As I write we are four months away from LEGO day and I genuinely have no idea how much bigger it will get before then. But what's clear is that it's already creating excitement, mainly amongst the adults it has to be said, and I simply cannot wait!

100 Club – This lottery style draw was launched in 2013 as a way of both fundraising and giving something back to members. A 'number', which costs £12 per year, is entered into a monthly draw with the chance to win one of three cash prizes. The prizes depend on how many are entered in each draw but 40 percent of the total is paid out to winners each month and 60 percent of the money benefits The Centre – in its first year the Club will have raised £1280 for The Centre and paid out £811 in prize money to the winners.

Three other Projects underway during the Anniversary Year are:

- **Refurbishment** – Over a period of 18–24 months The Centre will be undergoing a phased makeover:

  The Youth Area and Kitchen. The youth area is the first space people see when they come in. It will have some new furniture and a new toy corner with puzzles and children's books. We want to turn it into a comfortable and relaxing cafe-like area that young people can enjoy after school or at Youth Club or where others can enjoy a good quality cup of tea or coffee and a chat while their children play safely; and the kitchen will be up-graded to meet regular catering needs.

  The Juice Bar. This has been re-floored and will be made into a pleasant social space with a comfy sofa, coffee table, television and water cooler. With its viewing area to the Sports Hall, it can be used as a waiting area before a fitness class or just at any time.

  The Music Room. This room will be made into a better multi-functional space, brightened by the addition of a window. Music and recording facilities will be possible with the provision of a laptop with specialist recording software.

- **Anniversary Film** – This will be a 10-15 minute documentary-type film comprising footage taken over the Anniversary Year as well as material from previous years. Like the Book, it will tell the story of The Centre and also highlight many of the events and activities that happen within The Centre on a regular weekly and annual basis. It will be available to view online on The Centre's website and Facebook page and the film will be a useful means to help support funding applications.

- **Garden Project** – The garden and green spaces around The Centre are being developed to create safer access and better social spaces for everyone, particularly for our young people. This work is being planned in stages, beginning with the creation of a continuous path down the left hand side of the car park, allowing safer pedestrian access to The Centre entrance, and we intend to improve the garden area to the rear of the building by extending the space and having outdoor seating. On the grassed area to the right hand side of the building an orchard will be planted which will have a carpet of wild flowers and snowdrops.

One of the Garden Projects: The New Path - Before, During and After; The Garden Group and Helpers: (l-r) Rebekah Kittridge, Stewart Prodger, Andy McBroom, Pete Bicheno, Paul Jones, Susan Morris, Chelsea Ross, Sam Pilkington, Gemma Greer.

.. and, of course, this Book

... to which so many have contributed including those in the photos below at two of the many meetings when we shared our memories and experiences of The Centre.

Book Get-Togethers – April and May 2014.

Staff in the Anniversary Year – March 2014: (l-r) Helen McLaren, Lynn Balman, Barbara McPake, Teresa McQuaid, Deborah Forster, Louise Bleakley, Gemma Greer, Leigh Austin, John Nixon, Ryan Anderson.

A Graffiti Art Mural to Celebrate the Tenth Anniversary.

CHAPTER 9 – LOOKING TO THE FUTURE

STEVE BIRNIE and GEMMA GREER
with a contribution from HEATHER MACPHERSON

STEVE BIRNIE – CHAIRMAN OF THE CENTRE'S BOARD OF TRUSTEES

The book has focused so far on where the Dunblane Centre came from, the people who have been involved and the activities and successes of the past ten years. This chapter is an opportunity to explore what will happen next and for me to share my vision of what I hope the future holds.

Steve Birnie outside The Centre after carrying the Olympic Torch – 13 June 2012.

My involvement in the life of The Centre began during my first visit to the brand new building, made three days before the Opening Ceremony in September 2004. Our son Matthew was one of the children injured in the shootings at Dunblane Primary School in March 1996, and because of this personal connection I had been asked to The Centre to give some interviews for local media. Whilst there I became aware of the numerous boxes that had not been opened and of chairs still wrapped in cellophane. Once the interviews were over I rolled up my sleeves and started unwrapping chairs and setting up computers. And I've been involved ever since, joining the Board shortly afterwards and serving as chairman for the last eight years.

The trustees are a group of dedicated volunteers from a variety of backgrounds who give up their time to provide strategy and direction as well as practical support to the manager and staff. Over the ten years The Centre has been operating, and during the years prior to that when it was being planned and built, we have been fortunate to have so many extremely committed people as trustees and without their help and support The Centre would not have existed, let alone been able to succeed.

The Dunblane Centre Trustees – July 2014: (l-r) David Spooner, Martyn Dunn, Howard Barr, Gemma Beher, Steve Birnie, Stewart Prodger, Clare Moore and Gez Gourlay.

As a Board we have always been very conscious of the part that past events have played in shaping The Centre, and we remain passionate about ensuring that it continues to be a positive legacy for the local community. It is important for readers of this book to be aware that for its day-to-day operation The Centre has to be self-funding. The annual sum of £230,000 which is needed to keep the doors open must come primarily from our users. While we actively fundraise, with an excellent group of volunteers who help with this, and apply for grants for specific projects, it is only with the Community's support, through their use of the facilities and attendance at events and, critically, spreading the word to others that we can keep the legacy growing.

The balance of the funds held by the Dunblane Community Trust (DCT) (see Chapters 2-4) after the building of the Dunblane Centre had been completed was for the express purpose of long term maintenance and to provide support in the event of an emergency involving the fabric of the building. Following discussions with DCT it has been agreed that the trustees of the Dunblane Youth and Sports Centre Trust (DY&SCT) will take over the management of these funds. While the purpose of the funds is unchanged The Centre now has complete control over its investment and management. DCT also suggested that the DY&SCT trustees should take over ownership of the land on which The Centre is built, which will hopefully allow greater access to future grants and other funding opportunities. This has been a very welcome development during this special year, and it is antic-ipated that the legal details needed to allow this to happen will be completed before the end of 2014.

In December 2012 the DY&SCT Board agreed to adopt a strategy for the future which would:

- Ensure the Dunblane Centre is a facility the Community is proud to own
- Put The Centre even more at the heart of the Community by seeking to engage with the hearts and minds of those who currently do not use it
- Ensure The Centre provides a warm and welcoming environment, open to all and supporting the needs of everyone in the Community – to do this we will redesign and refresh some of our public areas to enhance their multi-purpose use
- Re-launch The Centre during this special tenth year, highlighting its charitable status and stressing its unique nature and legacy
- Aim for The Centre to trade at a profit so that any monies made can be re-invested into maintaining the building and developing the facilities

The Board also agreed a set of guiding principles which would help direct the future activities:

- Because of its history the major focus of The Centre should continue to be young people
- The Centre should continue to help youngsters explore and develop their potential
- The profitable activities of The Centre should subsidise the youth activities to ensure that the costs to young people and their families are kept to a minimum

- The Centre should act as a catalyst to break down barriers between young people and the rest of the community
- The Centre must be responsive to the wishes and needs of Dunblane and continue to engage actively with key community partners including schools, businesses, the police, the community council and other local voluntary organisations

So that The Centre can develop and grow we have to look at the changing needs of the Community. The population of Dunblane is expanding and a lot of people who have moved to the town have young families and school-age children. In the near future we plan to refresh the main drop-in area and make it a welcoming and safe place for mums, dads and grandparents to meet and have a cup of coffee whilst their children play. As we refresh and renovate The Centre, one space in particular will require special attention, the kitchen. Its facilities were never designed to support large-scale catering but we are now finding that providing catering is a significant element for many meetings and fundraising events, hence the need for improved facilities. We want to change the daytime atmosphere of The Centre, giving it a more relaxed, family-friendly coffee shop feel with home baking and good quality coffee. To achieve all of this our kitchen will be upgraded (see Chapter 8).

Older members of the Community are also important to The Centre, a place which should provide a welcome for them with activities that meet their interests and encourage them to be involved. We are exploring ideas such as tea dances, classic movie screenings, monthly luncheon clubs and the provision of courses and information afternoons on topics suggested by our senior members. One of our key aims is to break down the barriers between the generations, and one way we can do this is to get young people involved in many of these activities as well.

As is apparent elsewhere in the book, the performing arts and music play a huge part in the life of The Centre. This is sure to continue. Performing is a fantastic way for young people to build self-confidence, and each year, between the Panto and the Show in a Week, over 200 young people take to the stage. We want to continue to develop this key aspect of The Centre's life and will be looking at further opportunities to encourage members of all ages to participate. The launch of a community choir, its membership spanning the whole range from teenage to pension age, reflects this.

And to make it easier and more affordable to produce our highly successful shows we are looking at providing the Sports Hall with permanent rigging for lights and a more convenient system for changing the nets and the backdrops we use to section off the courts.

The Music Room with its recording studio is one of the many unique features offered by The Centre. It's a facility used by musicians of all ages and with every type of musical taste from folk to rock. There are music lessons, including pre-school music makers and guitar and drum classes. We have plans to acquire a new laptop-based recording system, available for anyone, which will make the process of recording music much easier (see Chapter 8).

The space outside the building is one we wish to exploit more as it gives us an opportunity to extend our legacy even further. We have plans to develop an Anniversary Orchard as a long lasting reminder of this tenth year. The apple crop will be harvested and pressed by the young people as an enjoyable learning experience. Towards the back of The Centre is a wooded area which we will convert into a safer and fun environment where young people can play and learn. We have nesting boxes with internal web cams, making it possible to observe eggs hatching and chicks growing. Within the plans there are outdoor play spaces and seating areas, allowing greater use of the outdoor space.

But we will also be looking beyond the actual site of The Centre. While plenty of young people are already using its facilities, we know there are others who pre-fer to be in a more unstructured environment. And so in future we intend to become more involved in outreach work by providing activities at the other local places where youngsters tend to meet.

We have links already with a number of community organisations and give support to the Dunblane Road Race by providing marshals and contribute to the High Street open evening every Christmas. Every summer The Centre hosts Dunblane 'Create', free summer activities organised by Stirling Council's Youth Services with whom we have very good relations.

Heather MacPherson, Operation Leader for Youth Services Education at Stirling Council, explains more about the collaboration

"Stirling Council Youth Services congratulates Dunblane Centre on its Tenth Anniversary. Over the years, Youth Services and Dunblane Centre have worked together on a number of projects which have enhanced learning and development opportunities for local young people.

"In recent years Dunblane Centre has hosted the 'Create' summer programme, with over 100 local young people attending each time. The Centre lends itself to be an excellent venue for the fun packed 'Create' programme and really enhances the experience of the young people taking part.

"Youth Services, Dunblane Centre and a number of other Community Planning Partners supported young people to actively participate in a Participatory Budgeting initiative aimed at reducing Anti Social Behaviour in local communities. The Dunblane Young Peoples' Project (DYPP) was one of five national pilot areas picked. The successful Saturday Night Project in The Centre was one of the projects funded as a result of the work DYPP undertook locally.

The DYPP Cheque, displayed by Jason and Sean Balman, presented to The Centre.

David Marquetty (l) with Aidan McGuire on a Centre Outing to Alton Towers – August 2013.

"Dunblane Centre was able to support Youth Services with providing a Modern Apprenticeship Opportunity for a young person from Stirling. David Marquetty worked as Youth Information and Café Worker in Dunblane Centre for approximately 18 months. David achieved his SVQ Level 2 and continues to work in The Centre supporting the evening youth group provision.

"Youth Services is keen to continue our positive and effective relationship with Dunblane Centre to ensure that opportunities for young people are relevant and of high quality. We are delighted to work in collaboration with Dunblane Centre and wish the trustees, staff, volunteers and young people all the very best in the future."

There is a close involvement with Dunblane First Responders whose public access defibrillator is now located in a wall-mounted cabinet within the porch of The Centre. Continued partnership and closer collaboration will be a significant part of our future. There is a personal reflection from Alan Nichols, a founder member who also runs the

Dunblane First Responders at The Centre.

Sports First Aid Training at The Centre, in Chapter 7.

As a symbol of the support given to the community of Dunblane from people all over the world The Centre has always been much more than a building. And what continues to make it even more 'special' is its people. Everyone who attends will tell you that there is a 'good feel' about the place, it's a positive environment, it brings people together. Once you've spent time at The Centre it gets under your skin.

Not long after I got involved, my wife Bev became a volunteer on the Events Committee and over the years must have made hundreds of cups of tea, not to mention the cakes and soups for many various community events. Bev also enjoys the keep fit classes. Our children Matt and Lauren both became young volunteers and Matt also worked in The Centre during his gap year (see Chapter 7). I am very proud of the logo that Lauren designed for the Tenth Anniversary which graces the front cover of this book. The Centre has enriched our family, and as for many other families in Dunblane, it is and will continue to be very much part of our lives. When you see the huge variety of users, from every age group, and the range of activities on offer you can start to understand why it is so important that with the Community's support, this gift, given by the world to Dunblane, must keep on growing.

Bev Birnie (r) serving Teas with Jan McClelland.

GEMMA GREER – DC MANAGER SINCE JUNE 2012

After spending most of my working life working with a Charity and Community Group I had moved away to work in the 'corporate world'. But I discovered pretty quickly that this wasn't me, and it was around this time that The Centre manager job came up. I was told about the position by someone else who wanted to apply but I found I was immediately drawn to it …. and talked him out of applying.

I knew The Centre. I had been there previously for youth activities and, for a short period during the early days, had been part of the netball group. But even though I knew a little of what went on, after my first interview I still wasn't sure whether I could actually take on the job. During the recruitment process I had attended an event at The Centre and quizzed the staff, Andrew and Michelle, who were unaware that I'd applied. It wasn't until I was asked back to a 'meet and greet' with staff, volunteers, trustees and instructors that I realised how much I did want this job. The stories I heard, the people I met and all the kindness they showed made me want to be part of this special team and this unique place.

That evening was the first time I met Nancy McLaren. She talked me into coming along to the Race Night in a few weeks time - I even got a phone call two weeks later, 'just to remind me'. That was my first experience of 'you never say no to Nancy' (see Chapter 7).

I will never forget my first day – no clue what to expect or what I was doing. For the first few weeks it was tough trying to remember all the activities, but everyone was amazing. I loved chatting to all the fitness ladies and getting to know the kids, and the staff team was and still is great! I'm a real people person and that's what I love about my job. I love having a 'wee blether' with people when they come into The Centre or after they've finished a class. I'm shocking with names, but after two years I think I finally know most people. Even though I don't live in Dunblane it's great to walk around the town or attend a fun day at the school or a Dunblane Fling and recognise people and stop for a chat. It's working at The Centre which has done that. I really love those community days out.

117

Gemma Greer talking to BBC TV.

One of my most favourite days, one that encapsulated the special combination of working and socialising that I get from The Centre, was around my birthday, which always coincides with Wimbledon. In 2013 it was the day of Andy Murray's semi-final. I had been working during the day, trying to get everything cleared up before heading off on holiday the next day and then staying on to watch the game. All the staff had planned a surprise get-together with cake and presents in the afternoon. It was completely overwhelming and I was so taken aback that they had done this for me (it was a special birthday). And afterwards there was the tennis. The Centre was busy with lots of people and a crowd of us went and got Chinese food to eat whilst we watched. I loved how I could be at work but be completely social and relaxed, even though the match itself, as with all of Andy's, was very tense. It was a really fun night and of course Andy won. Two days later The Centre hosted a huge and enthusiastic crowd to watch the Final, but I was gutted as I had travelled home to Ireland and missed Andy's phenomenal win! Never before had I wanted to be in two different places at the same time so much.

As other contributors to the book have described, Show in a Week is a stressful but fabulous event (see Chapter 6 and Chapter 7). Its imminent arrival is always interesting – I try to avoid Pamela in the run-up as every time I see her she'll be telling me "another one for Show in a Week". That's one more budding child star signed up ahead of a wonderful on-stage experience. For the 2014 show, 'Oliver' we had 136 eager youngsters in the wings, raring to go and be involved. It's an incredible week. At the start no one knows anything, and by the end of the first day it's too easy to think "seriously how are they going to pull this off!?" But the anticipation builds up as the week goes on. The stage arrives and gets dressed, the lights go up, the props and back drops appear … and then by the Friday evening I'm filled with huge pride as I watch the kids from the back of the Hall.

The Future

The Tenth Anniversary represents a key stage in the life of The Centre and an important opportunity to reflect on its potential. There are so many things I want to achieve but just not enough hours in the day, even when I can be, and have been, at The Centre twelve hours in a day and not even realised it. Here is how I view the future:

- I am very keen for The Centre to cater for every age group with activities for everyone in the community from the most junior to the most senior. Our pre-school and youth programmes are great and offer so much, but we lack activities for our older members, especially those who are retired. I hope The

Centre will be able to offer more for them in future. We certainly have the potential to provide our older members with a variety of opportunities on a daily basis. The Centre should be a place for meeting others with similar interests.

- I would love all young people to be able to access The Centre as cheaply as possible and hope we can aim to achieve this. This is a facility planned with its focus on young people. The activities, events and classes all support the youth programme, but wouldn't it be great if funding was organised so that cost was no barrier to any young person?

- Our pre-school programme has gone from strength to strength and I want to continue to see this grow and develop. Being a new parent can be scary and frightening, but The Centre can continue to be a place where mums and dads are able to relax by finding support, meeting other parents and sharing stories and experiences.

- In keeping with our wish to provide for all of the Dunblane community we have plans to widen the scope of our adult activities. There are already a number of well attended fitness classes and a community choir, and the Art Room has great facilities for adult art classes. The Centre can offer something for everyone and every hobby.

Gemma Greer and her fiancé Neil Connell
(who is also a Volunteer) at the 2013
Tartan Ball.

I feel so privileged to be part of the team and am proud to be involved at this key stage in The Centre's life. My position as manager has already given me so much – I love coming to work. We have a great team and The Centre is a truly unique place. I can't believe how fast these last two years have gone – I'd better stop telling people I'm new! The Centre is the kind of place that consumes you, it has drawn me in and I can't help but care deeply about it.

CHAPTER 10 – REFLECTIONS

MICK NORTH, NORA GILFILLAN and PAM ROSS

A WAY FORWARD

Nora, who at the time was a member of the Dunblane Primary School Board, reflects on a conversation she had in March 1996 and which, for her, sowed a seed for recovery:

> "Mrs Eadington, the deputy head of Dunblane Primary in 1996, spoke to me outside the church after the funeral for one of the children. She said that we must not let 'him' win and destroy our town and we should build a place for children to play and feel safe. At a time when I felt so cold and sad her words made an impression on me, not least because they gave me hope at a very dark time and showed me that there was a way forward.

> "Therefore, it seemed an appropriate way to use the funds set aside for community use to build a youth-focussed centre. Eight years later in September 2004 the Dunblane Centre opened its doors, and now the gift would grow and become a living tribute to the children and Mrs Mayor. That was an exciting day, a very positive and proud day. The support given to our project was unprecedented; the vision of a dedicated fun-filled but safe environment for the children and the young people had become a reality. Someone commented at the Opening that The Centre was like a 'Phoenix rising from the Ashes'.

> "Prior to The Centre opening, like most things around the planning there was much discussion about what the name should be – and the consensus was not to call it the Community Centre – perhaps we thought that would be too presumptuous. However, something wonderful happened and The Centre did become the centre for the Community as hundreds of users and volunteers started to become part of it.

> "I feel that not only do we have a wonderful and unique facility which is funded and supported by the local community through its various activities but that with this support everyone involved is enabling youth work. At a time when so many children and young people only connect through social media, The Centre is bringing our local children together in 'real socialising', chatting and playing in a safe and healthy environment. Dunblane is a good place to bring up our children – we have not forgotten what happened nor how The Centre came about, however we are honouring the memory of those who died at Dunblane Primary School by nurturing and caring for our present and future generations of children and young people.

> "Something very good has come from something very bad."

OUR THOUGHTS

As we prepared this book we had the privilege and pleasure of gathering to-gether a wealth of memories and reflections from those who have contributed to the success of the Dunblane Centre. These contributions have been enhanced by the many photographic images from an important and poignant period in the town's history. Our only disappointment has been that it was possible to include just a small proportion of the material available to us.

There were many reasons for wanting to record this history. What better way could there be to celebrate an important milestone in the life of The Centre, its Tenth Anniversary, than by publishing an account of how the idea for The Centre was conceived and developed and of how the project was successfully completed and now supports a range of activities from which so many people, young and old, benefit. We wanted the folk of Dunblane to know how well the gift they received in 1996 continues to grow eighteen years on. And it was also as important to create something special through which we could send a 'thank you' message to all those who gave so generously in response to the Tragedy and without whom this project would never have been possible. We want them to know how their money has helped to provide a lasting and positive legacy to Dunblane. When they responded in 1996 they let us know that Dunblane's children and teachers would always be remembered, and we now want to show to them that their kindness is something that we have never forgotten.

From the contributions made to this book there is no doubt about the importance of The Centre. One very special message emerges throughout and that is, that after a tragic event as devastating as the one that took place at our local primary school, nothing reflects better the strength and recovery of the town than the achievements of the Dunblane Centre.

In working on the book we were not just editors. Each of us had our own very personal involvement in the events of 13 March 1996. For everyone who was close to the Tragedy there were many things that would be of critical importance during the immediate aftermath, not least the need for continuing support for those most affected, and for openness, ongoing consultation and clarity of purpose about anything being undertaken that was linked to what happened at the Primary School. It was also going to be essential that these aims remained at the forefront of any future projects. And it is to the credit of all those involved that as the Dunblane Centre took shape these essentials remained at the heart of every step in the process.

As is recalled in the earlier chapters the steps that led to the building and opening of The Centre were lengthy and sometimes tortuous, but they were ultimately successful. We believe that there are many positive lessons that can be learnt from the processes involved and that these lessons extend well beyond Dunblane and its own tragedy. They provide a fine example of how a community, with the help of countless others from outside the town, can deal with and recover from its darkest hour.

We commend and salute all those who over the years were able to steer around and negotiate the difficulties, tensions and pitfalls which might have prevented the Dunblane Centre becoming a reality. Through a series of sensitive processes those involved ensured that the goodwill that flooded into the town during 1996 has culminated in the development of such a positive symbol of recovery, and there is little doubt that the processes that worked best were those in which as many people as possible were involved and consulted.

One person with a key role in the project, its architect **Willie Brown**, made these post-contract observations in 2005. They remain pertinent and reflect not only the importance of what he and his colleagues achieved but undoubtedly encapsulate the thoughts of many others who had been involved:

"It was felt inappropriate to seek any further outside funding to complement the donations received from all over the world after the tragedy, so tight cost control was a priority from the outset, and it is pleasing to be able to report that the project was delivered within the budget.

The Centre during Construction.

"There is no doubt that the project elicited a strong emotional response from all who worked on it.

"The huge feeling of goodwill and unstinting effort from the engineers, quantity surveyor, contractors, glaziers who produced the sandblasted images, even site neighbours Dunblane Bowling Club, made the delivery of a complex building on a tight sloping site much easier than it could have been.

"Looking back 8 years to when we started working up a brief with the Youth Project committee, I do not think that we would have done anything differently, the process had to take the time it did to allow a clarity of thought from client and designers alike, that would have been difficult in the immediate aftermath of the Tragedy."

POSITIVE LESSONS

We wanted to reflect further on some of those key factors which we consider helped to make the Dunblane Centre the success it has become. These, we believe, can offer valuable guidance to others who find themselves having to deal with the aftermath and legacy of tragic events.

The Brand New Centre – 2004.

When such an event, and especially one involving children, hits the headlines it is inevitable that many of those watching their TV screens or reading news reports will want to respond, feeling a need to do something. Often this is a desire simply to send money. Such donations may be prompted by formal appeals, but not always, and the fact that many of them are made spontaneously reflects a kindness coming from the heart of our fellow human beings. They are a means for a wider community to reach out and try to connect with those who have suffered in a way that they themselves are struggling to comprehend. People want to show they care, and in the absence of such caring responses humanity would undoubtedly be diminished. There is little doubt that the gifts donated by a generous public can be hugely beneficial both to those directly involved and to the wider community.

However, the sudden influx of gifts, especially those of money, can bring difficulties. We know, not only from experiences in Dunblane but following other tragedies, that support from outside is not always received with unmitigated gratitude, especially as it happens at a time of stress and tension to people who have yet to come to terms with why something so awful has happened in their community. The gifts can, in fact, feel like an additional burden with the potential to disturb rather than enhance the healing process. They can cause splits when differences of opinion emerge as to how the donations can be used. That should not be so, and we believe it is essential, however difficult it might prove to be at the time, that the manner of receiving should match the generosity of the giving.

From the earliest days many of us in Dunblane had supported the idea of a single fund for donations. Such a fund would have allowed all decisions to be made in an objective and non-partisan way and helped to ensure an appropriate balance between the needs and wishes of the Families and the Community. Although a single fund did not emerge in Dunblane, the subsequent creation of the Dunblane Community Trust (DCT), which received the money remaining in the two major funds, did provide a single source of funding which allowed the Dunblane Centre project to go ahead. By this time immediate support for the victims and victims' families had been met and key projects of remembrance, such as the creation of the Memorial Garden, had been completed. The most trusted funds, including DCT, were able to draw on professional help, in this case provided by the local authority. The need for such help along with objectivity, particularly necessary to avoid potential vested interests within a small community, cannot be overemphasised.

The choice of a community project for Dunblane took time, and perhaps one of the most important factors that helped the ultimate success of The Centre was that this major decision had not been taken too quickly. Nothing had hurt the families of the victims more than finding out, just a few short weeks after their loved ones had been killed and injured, that the Community was rushing to decide how to spend a windfall which had only come to the town because of what happened to the children and teachers. Whilst it was important to ensure that the donors' wishes to help support the victims and their families were met as soon as possible, there was no similar urgency with community projects. For the townsfolk things could wait, and although it was not a deliberate decision to take as long as eight years before the completion of The Centre, the wait, nevertheless, helped ensure that adequate consultation had taken place during which any mis-understandings could be resolved.

Some of us have had the sad privilege of sharing experiences with special people from other communities around the world who have lost loved ones in circumstances similar to Dunblane. Those most directly affected always feel over-whelmed in the immediate aftermath, unable at the time to participate in decisions which, nevertheless, should still involve them. It is hardly surprising that different groups within a community will recover at different rates, but those most affected must never be left out. We have heard too often of victims' families feeling they are being sidelined as others try to move on too quickly. One of the main lessons, exemplified by what happened in Dunblane, is to take account of the time that's needed and the reflective thought required before undertaking something as important and sensitive as a major community project. To respect those who have lost most, it is imperative that some decisions should wait until all are well on the path to recovery so that everyone is able to participate in the process if they wish to do so.

Those involved with the Dunblane Centre project did make sure that consultation was paramount and that both the victims' families and the Community as a whole could feel a part of the project. Consultation with the Community was achieved through discussion with as many individuals and groups as possible, especially those concerned with youth work, through invitations to the meetings at which a Youth Project was first discussed and through a survey sent to everyone in the town. And the Community was also represented by the trustees of DCT whose decision to fund the project allowed The Centre to go ahead.

It was also essential that the project had the support of those closest to the Tragedy. It is inevitable that those who have lost loved ones and then watch as money is donated because of their loss will have a heightened sensitivity about how that money is used. Sadly, it is sometimes possible for a community to ignore these feelings and leave the families marginalised. When in 1997 the first meeting was planned to discuss proposals for a Youth Centre in Dunblane the organisers made sure that an invitation was made for a representative of the bereaved parents to attend. That invitation led to Les Morton's key involvement with the Youth Centre and the Dunblane Centre for many years. This link was essential, because at that time many of the families were very wary of the funds being used for a bricks-and-mortar project in the town. The knowledge that the new Centre would be focussing on youth activities helped persuade many of us to lend our support. Once the idea for The Centre had gelled and as the plans for the new building began to take shape the Families were kept informed about what was happening throughout and given opportunities to see the building during construction.

The Centre was not built as a formal memorial to the Dunblane victims, there are many other memorials in the town. But it had to be in keeping with a tribute to them and its origins represented in some way. Those references are subtle. The designs for the personalised windows will always be a poignant but low key reminder of why The Centre is there. The Families were included throughout the selection process. Those using The Centre don't have constant reminders of what happened at the Primary School, but we hope the Community never forgets the reason it is there and has become an important feature of Dunblane's life. The links to the events of 13 March 1996 may not always be obvious but they will always be part of The Centre.

Many of the families affected by the events at Dunblane Primary School participate in the life of The Centre. We are involved as volunteers, staff, trustees and patron. And each year on the Anniversary, family members gather to light candles in memory of their children and their teacher.

The gifts received by Dunblane in 1996 were used in many ways. Some provided financial support to the survivors and the families of all the victims and funded special activities for many of those most closely affected. Donations were used to create memorials such as the garden at Dunblane Cemetery and stained glass windows at local churches. There are sculptures and benches around the town in memory of the victims. These legacies are permanent reminders of what happened in March 1996.

But as a community project the Dunblane Centre is different. It is very much a gift for the whole community of Dunblane and one which belongs to the Community. The Centre was created through donations made by countless individual donors, many of whose names are not known. With the exception of the grant from **sport**scotland there was no single major donor and so no organisation or corporation can lay claim to ownership or take credit for The Centre. Thanks to all the support the town received in 1996, the ownership and credit are Dunblane's. The Centre stands on its own, a part of the Community for whom it was an unconditional gift.

Most importantly, The Centre is a gift that has had the capacity to grow, its future continually being shaped by the Community which uses it. It's a community of all ages but we are delighted that the focus remains on youth and that the children and young people of Dunblane will continue to benefit for a long time from 'The Gift That Keeps Growing'.

FINAL REFLECTION

The most fitting way for this book to conclude is with the following words from Pam, who works at The Centre and whose daughter Joanna was one of the young victims in March 1996:

"So much of what I feel about The Centre has already been said in different ways throughout this book. What else could I add?

"This place holds very special meaning and countless special memories to different people in all sorts of ways, so I'd like to share how I came to feel the way I do about the Dunblane Centre.

"For a long time after 13 March 1996 I was really quite opposed to and had certain misgivings about the proposed project that was to become the Dunblane Centre, let alone ever consider the idea of working there. Dunblane

had long been overlooked for a facility of this kind, and now suddenly, out of this overwhelming devastation, it seemed like the town had struck gold. The thought of its very existence only served to emphasise our loss.

"However, I also understood that the love and thoughtfulness of so many people here in Dunblane, throughout the country and across the world had offered an opportunity to turn such remarkable generosity into something which could become a very worthwhile reality. It wasn't an easy change of heart, but over time and through being persuaded by Nora to come and see the building during its construction and find out about the ideas going into it, I began to realise that something good could be created; something that my other children, and eventually grandchildren, could benefit from and that would be a permanent, useful and living tribute to my daughter Joanna, all her classmates and her teacher Gwen Mayor. Since it opened in September 2004, the Dunblane Centre has thrived and grown within the community – probably beyond most people's expectations – and has certainly grown on me.

"In 2006, when the company I worked for were moving their office out of Dunblane, the opportunity of a part-time job came up at The Centre. As a parent who had been directly affected, my perspective, connection and under-standing would be different, so I decided to apply and find out for myself what being involved there could be like and if I could offer something in return to those who had made it possible and those who would share in its future. My privilege has been to see at first hand the commitment, enthusiasm and enjoyment of the people at the very heart of it. Without the incredible vision and willingness of all those involved in its beginnings, along with the army of volunteers and supporters, young and old, patrons, trustees, manager, staff, instructors and users who all make it happen, this Centre could not be the success that it is.

"I love talking to everyone I meet and especially getting to know about them and what brings them into The Centre. As volunteer co-ordinator it would be great to be able to meet and know them all individually, but with so many volunteers, it just isn't possible. We all continue to be inspired by the skill, creativity and readiness they offer and I'd like to say a personal and heartfelt thank you to everyone who gives their time to supporting and helping.

"Reading so many of the stories here has reinforced my belief that the Centre represents more than just a building. Although I was already aware of how much the Centre means to lots of people, I was really encouraged and delighted to discover just how diverse and positive an effect it has had in so many instances. During its first ten years it has helped enrich, shape and direct the lives of many of those who have been part of it. It embodies all the good that was shown to our families and the wider Dunblane community, and our hope is that for a very long time to come it will continue to keep giving something back to the people who share its ambitions and benefit from all it provides.

"Although we can never know of every act of kindness that combined to create it, we want the world to know that we will always be mindful of how much we owe to each and every person who contributed then, and continue to do so in whatever way. We should always remember how and why it came to be here. The Dunblane Centre has a unique origin and is a very special gift to us all – a gift which deserves to be respected, appreciated and supported, but above all, enjoyed. Out of the loss, despair and pain of 1996, it is evidence of something truly positive and I am very proud and fortunate to be part of it. Thank you."

"Come and meet us. Share some of its special appeal.
It's yours. Please keep it growing."

Reflections –
'Forever Remembered'.

Candles lit at The Centre
on the Anniversary of the
Dunblane Tragedy.

'Out of Darkness into Light'

ACKNOWLEDGEMENTS

Reflecting The Centre itself this book would never have been possible without the participation of many people from Dunblane and elsewhere. Their recollections during chats and conversations and their written contributions and photos have been invaluable. We are especially grateful to Dunblane hero Andy Murray, our Patrons Lord Robertson and Lord Forsyth, Stan Bradley, Les Morton, Willie Brown, Scott Neil, Andy McBroom, Bob Dale, Pamela Mackie, Nancy McLaren, Steve Birnie and Gemma Greer and to everyone else whose words have helped put the story and life of The Centre on the pages of this book. We would also like to thank Allan Rennie and James Matthews for their help in providing photographs from media archives and to everyone else who has allowed us to use their images.

We are delighted to include Lauren Birnie's stunning Tenth Anniversary logo in the Cover design.

We are greatly indebted to the JJ Munro Charitable Trust for providing a grant to support the publication of this book and to Gordon Robertson and all the staff at Monument Press for the tremendous help they have given us to ensure that our amateur editorial team could produce a professional book.

The success of the Dunblane Centre would never have been possible without the support of friends and local businesses, many of whom we've not had the opportunity to mention, and so it would be appropriate to take this opportunity to acknowledge our appreciation to everyone and anyone who has contributed to that success.

Finally we'd like to thank all our own friends and family who have supported us as we have worked on the book over the past year.

Mick North, Pam Ross and Nora Gilfillan

August 2014